THE
INTIMATE
GARDEN

ALSO BY GORDON HAYWARD

Garden Paths

Taylor's Weekend Gardening Guide: Paths

Stone in the Garden

Your House, Your Garden

THE
INTIMATE
GARDEN

Twenty Years and
Four Seasons
in Our Garden

GORDON HAYWARD
AND MARY HAYWARD

WITH PHOTOGRAPHS BY
RICHARD W. BROWN

W. W. Norton & Company
New York • London

For information about permission to reproduce selections from this book, write to Permissions, W. W. Norton & Company, Inc., 500 Fifth Avenue, New York, NY 10110

Manufacturing by R.R. Donnelley, Roanoke Division
Book design by Susan McClellan
Production manager: Julia Druskin

Library of Congress Cataloging-in-Publication Data

Hayward, Gordon.
The intimate garden : twenty years and four seasons in our garden / Gordon Hayward and Mary Hayward ; with photographs by Richard W. Brown.
    p. cm.
  Includes index.
  ISBN 0-393-05893-X (hardcover)
 1. Hayward, Gordon—Homes and haunts—Vermont—Westminster—
Anecdotes. 2. Hayward, Mary—Homes and haunts—Vermont—
Westminster—Anecdotes. 3. Landscape gardening—Vermont—
Westminster—Anecdotes. 4. Gardens—Vermont—Westminster—Design—
Anecdotes. I. Hayward, Mary. II. Title.
    SB455.H37 2005
    712'.6'097439—dc22
                                            2004026994

W. W. Norton & Company, Inc.
500 Fifth Avenue, New York, N.Y. 10110
www.wwnorton.com

W. W. Norton & Company Ltd.
Castle House, 75/76 Wells Street, London W1T 3QT

1 2 3 4 5 6 7 8 9 0

Dedication

WE DEDICATE THIS BOOK TO THE RANNEY FAMILY, who, more than two hundred years ago, built the house we live in and cleared the woods to make the meadows we look out on. Through our neighbors Harold and Joyce Ranney, their late son Gary, their son Philip, his wife Teah, and their son Garrett, the Ranneys continue to look after their farm and the beautiful landscape that surrounds our garden.

CONTENTS

Mary's Acknowledgments

I WOULD LIKE TO THANK my mother, Phyllis Jones, and my grandmother Ellen Creber, both of whom in their quiet way instilled in me from early childhood a love of growing things. Gardening was as natural and necessary as breathing to them. And I owe a debt of gratitude to my father, Albert Jones, a man of quiet dignity, a farmer, who passed on to me his love and care for the land. I feel blessed to have grown up on our farm with its flower, fruit, and vegetable gardens in Hidcote Boyce in the Cotswold Hills of England. Most of all I wish to thank my husband, Gordon, who makes all things possible, who is a wonderful companion and friend.

Gordon's Acknowledgments

AS I WAS GROWING UP among the peach, apple, and pear trees in our orchard in Connecticut, my parents, John and Helen Hayward, taught me by example to appreciate the beauty of the natural world. My grandmother, Mabel Downing Hayward, my uncle Gordon, and our neighbor Ralph Blaikie were the first to show me the beauty of the ornamental garden. And it is my wife, Mary, my muse, whose love has made this life and this garden-making such a deep and abiding pleasure.

Our Acknowledgments

FIRST, WE WANT TO THANK the late David Reed, the previous owner of our Vermont house and land; he had faith in us and felt we would take good care of both. With the property in hand, we started the twenty-year journey in our garden with the help of the late Howard Andros and Dymock Maurice, whose spirits and plants are still with us. As we developed our garden, many people helped with its maintenance. We would especially like to thank Laura Cassidy, Kim Axsmith, Ayars Hemphill, Tracey Collins and Josh Clague, Robin Garlick, Siena MacFarland, and Pat Sanzone.

We also want to acknowledge the help that Chris and Jane Gooding provided in our garden in the Cotswolds followed by the work of Paul Williams as well as David Gunnell and his maintenance crew. Thanks to all of them, our garden in England gives us huge pleasure.

We would also like to acknowledge our son, Nathaniel, who grew up as we three were making both gardens; he is now embarking on his own life of growing plants in California.

Our garden, of course, led to this book, and we give our sincere thanks to John Barstow, our editor, who has offered us his enthusiasm, wise counsel, and encouragement. We also want to thank photographers Richard W. Brown in Vermont and Andrew Lawson, in England; Elayne Sears, for her lucid drawings; Kit Ward, our agent; Emily Ragsdale, who helped us choose the title *The Intimate Garden*; and Susan McClellan, who designed this beautiful book.

Introduction

WHEN MARY, OUR SON, NATE, AND I began creating our garden here in Vermont in early spring 1984, we were not doing much more than putting one foot in front of the other. Mary and I had been gardening individually all our lives, and together since we were married in 1976, but this was our first serious effort at making a one-and-a-half-acre garden to live in. As if that wasn't enough, we built a second teeny garden next to our cottage in the Cotswold Hills of England near where Mary grew up.

Even though your garden is different from ours, even though you garden in a different region, climate, soil, neighborhood, or hardiness zone (we're in Zone 4), even though your gardening style is different from ours, the design ideas we explore in this book will help you see ways to develop your own garden. To make this book truly useful, keep your own garden in mind. When we write about how we changed the shape of a lawn to fit better with the gardens around it, think about areas of your lawn that need reshaping. When we write about placing a garden ornament at the end of a straight path, think about your own straight paths. If you apply our twenty years of experience in your garden, you'll get where you're headed a lot sooner than we did.

Yet our gardens are clearly not the only ones you can learn from. To help you take the central idea of this book further, here are some questions to ask yourself when you visit a garden, because, in a way, reading this book is like visiting our garden. Your answers to these questions will help you understand design ideas at work in other people's gardens, ideas that you can take home and put to work with your own spade.

Relationship of House to Garden

HOUSES CAN BE SET within a garden or at the edge of it, or not even be visible from it. When you visit gardens, pay attention to how the house relates to the garden. Ask yourself the following questions.

- Is the approach to the front door apparent?
- What indicates the path to the front door?
- Do doors open to important paths? Do certain windows focus attention on specific views?
- How do exterior siding and trim materials relate to materials used in the garden? Do both have similarly painted surfaces, or brick, stone, or wooden surfaces?
- How do the proportions of beds and paved sitting areas near the house relate to the proportions of the house itself?

Once you understand the relationship between house and garden, you can consider the layout of the entire property. Public gardens often offer maps. Find north and orient yourself to the four points of the compass. This will help you understand plant choices and a vast range of other decisions related to sun and shade.

We give you maps of our two gardens (pages 16–17) and a quick walk through our Vermont garden in Chapter 1. If a map is available for the garden you are visiting, and it seems appropriate, take a fast-paced walk through the entire garden. But first, ask if there is an intended route you should

follow. Then, consider the following questions:

- Is there an entrance garden, and does it link the house to the main garden?
- Are all subsequent garden areas linked together by paths flowing from one area to the next, or is the progression confusing?
- Does the garden layout cause you to wander, or is it easy to follow an intended itinerary?
- Is the garden a single open space, with one area virtually indistinguishable from the next, or are there garden rooms and separate areas?
- Do separate garden areas appear as isolated islands in a sea of lawn, or are they visually and physically linked by paths and other elements that create cohesion?

An important element of a garden is its relation to the larger landscape. As you walk through the garden, notice the relationship of the garden proper to the world beyond.

- Is the garden enclosed and separate from its surroundings? If so, what materials or plants effect that separation?
- Or do views, vistas, and paths link the garden to the larger landscape? If so, do plants, benches, paths, or other garden elements draw

you from the garden into the surrounding woods, meadows, or neighborhood?

Clarify the Role of Each Area

ONCE YOU HAVE SEEN the whole garden, go back to the beginning. Take a more measured look as you walk through the garden a second time following the same route. To help understand the relationship between the whole and its parts, imagine the whole garden as being designed by one person, with each area representing a separate aspect of his or her personality. You could do the same with the gardens in this book.

- How are different garden areas used? Are some meant for sitting and others for strolling? Are some for outdoor entertainment and others for appreciating color and texture contrasts?
- How do sun, shade, and therefore temperature change from area to area?
- Are bed edges straight or curved? Do curved bed edges curve for a reason—around a tree, boulder, or large shrub—or do they just curve for the sake of curving?
- What fragrances are you aware of as you walk through each area of the garden?
- What is the relationship of lawn shape to bed shape? Are the two related and in proportion, or is the bed too small for the lawn?
- Do some garden areas feel too big (and too demanding) and others feel pinched and confining?
- If the garden has a water feature, does it excite or calm emotion? Does it produce sound or remain silent? Notice how water is used in each area.

Transitions

GOOD GARDEN DESIGN takes advantage of transitions between one garden area and the next. Gates, doorways, arbors, pergolas, a pair of standing stones, or a break in a wall or hedge are just a few ways to mark transitions. Another is to place planted pots or ornaments on stepping-stones, gravel, brick, stone, or any number of other materials. Pay attention to how transition zones are handled, for you may want to build them into your own garden.

- Are transition areas highlighted, or do they blend indistinctly into one another?
- Do steps or ramps mark transitions? If so, what materials are used?
- What do you see from the top and bottom steps as you go both up and down? The grander the steps, the grander the view you should see from the top. The top of a set of stairs is an important transition point; it directs the visitor's view in two directions.
- Do straight paths visually link one area to another by allowing a view from one area into the next, or are sight lines closed with doors or hedges?

Structures and Architecture

BUILT STRUCTURES, such as pergolas, gazebos, or arbors, act as visual magnets—destinations—that draw you along an itinerary. They also offer intimate spaces from which to look out at gardens, vistas, or views. Upright supports, doorways, or windows also frame views out across the garden and beyond. Garden structures ought to be built of materials and in a style that is appropriate to the garden. When you visit gardens, take time to sit on benches and chairs and look closely at how the garden's design directs your eye.

■ What are the garden's architectural elements?
■ How were their sites chosen?
■ Are the views from them commensurate with the structures?
■ What plants grow on or around structures to help them settle into the landscape?

Plant Choices

ONCE YOU UNDERSTAND the design and layout of a garden, begin to focus on the plants. Look at individual plants as well as how they have been used to create distinctive garden areas, each different from the others. Try to determine how plant choice and layout together establish the mood in each area of the garden.

■ What are the structure plants in a garden bed—the dominant trees, shrubs, or large perennials such as ornamental grasses that are repeated to provide continuity?
■ What plants fill in the spaces between the structure plants?
■ Is the focus on a certain bloom period or color theme?
■ Are there dominant colors, foliage shapes, or types of plants for certain soils or light conditions?

■ What colors predominate? Do you see areas where a dominant color and echoes of it are apparent?
■ Are trees used as individual specimens, repeated elements, architectural forms, or natural elements? Is there a wide variety of trees in the garden, or do certain ones predominate?
■ Does the garden style seem stiff and formal or relaxed and informal? The former may necessitate high maintenance and rigorous deadheadings; the latter tends to require less maintenance.

Once you have visited several gardens, you can make use of all your observations by looking back at your photos and notes. Choose one problem you're trying to solve in your garden (for example, where to put an arbor, how to make transitions from one area to the next, how to use a specific perennial or shrub in a border, or how to site garden ornaments). Then look back at your notes to compare how the same problems were solved in the other gardens. Through the process of comparison, you'll be able to put your garden visiting experience to use. Now let's take a quick walk through our U.S.D.A. Zone 4 garden in southern Vermont.

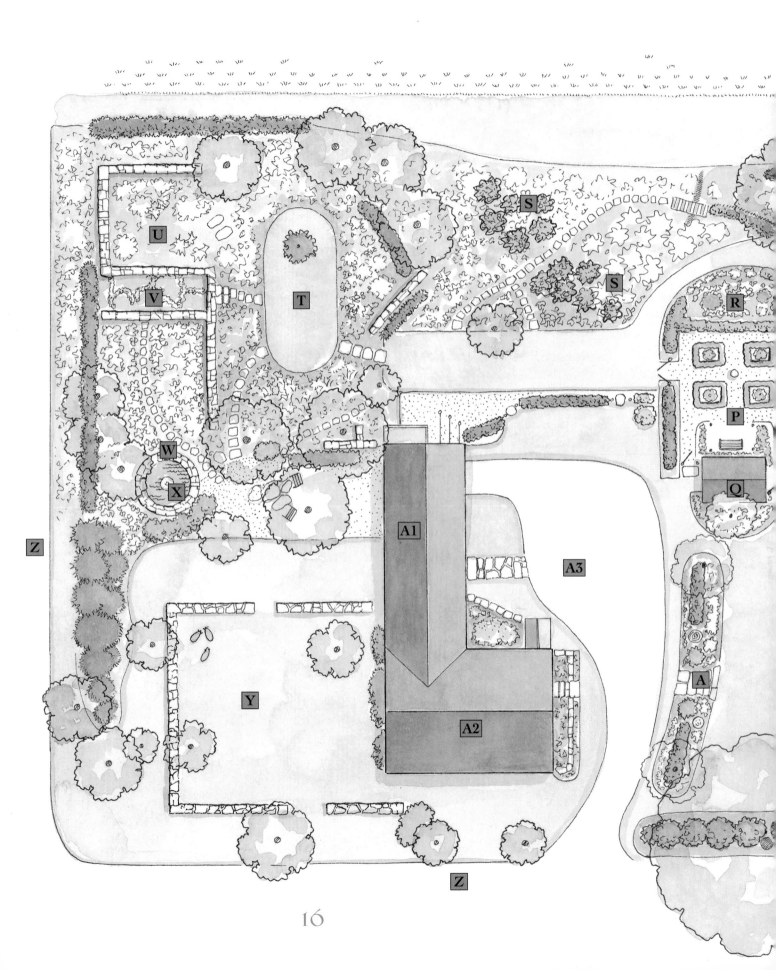

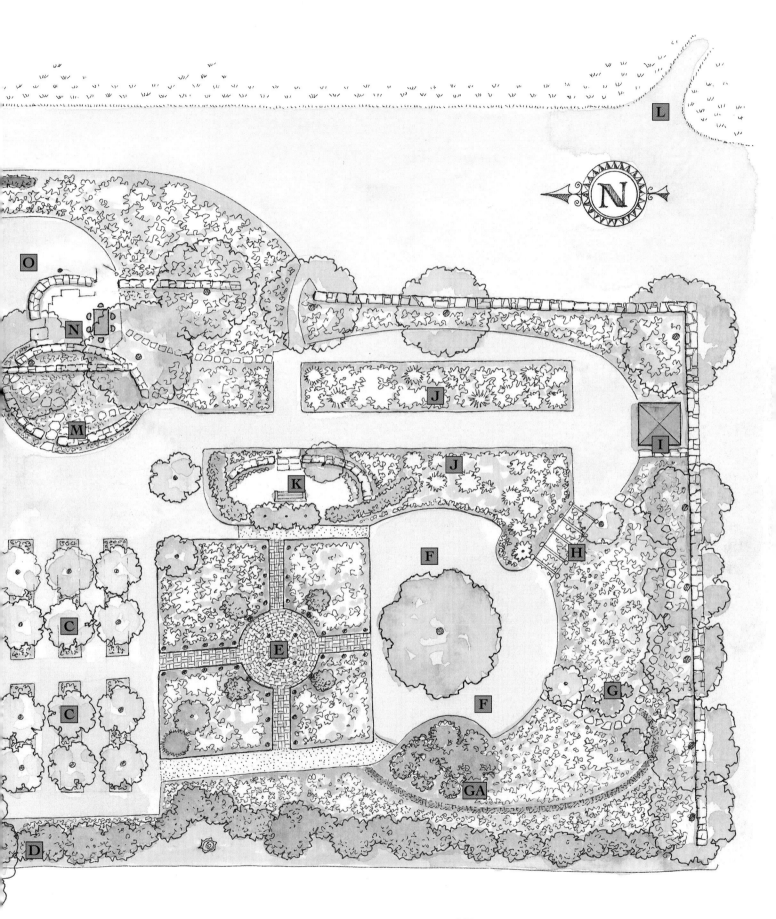

THE
INTIMATE
GARDEN

1

The Whole Garden

ONE SUNDAY AFTERNOON IN APRIL 1984, after living the first winter in our run-down farmhouse, my mentor, Howard Andros—then well into his seventies—dropped by for a visit. Howard had spent his life in gardens. Starting from the age of eleven, he walked from his home in Jamaica Plain, Massachusetts, to the nearby Arnold Arboretum on Sunday mornings to join E. H. "Chinese" Wilson, then curator of The Arnold, on his Sunday morning tours. Howard became a landscape designer and practiced in southern New Hampshire for forty-five years. Over a period of a year and a half, he shared his knowledge with me during two-hour Sunday morning meetings in his parlor and garden. When Howard spoke, I listened. This was a man of substance.

As Howard and his wife, Marion, walked with Mary, Nate, and me around the mess that would become our 1½-acre garden that April afternoon, he didn't say much. As we walked, he saw great potential for the garden, anchored as it was around the beautifully proportioned 200-plus-year-old farmhouse at the north end of a long, narrow, flat piece of ground. But he also saw the work ahead of us: removing three rusted hulks of cars long abandoned, uprooting half an acre of brambles and maple saplings, hauling away rotten nylon rugs the previous owner had used to mulch a vegetable garden, and removing what would be seven pickup truck loads of scrap metal. He also knew we were undaunted.

After our walk around the property, we were all standing by

the front door saying good-bye when Howard looked at the south-facing door of our house, then at an old apple tree some 250 feet due south of it. In his reticent New England manner, he said, "That's an important line." Then he and Marion were gone.

Given our years of experience visiting English gardens, with their strong use of the main door of the house to generate the primary path straight into the heart of the garden, we knew exactly what Howard meant, though we hadn't seen the line through the junk cars and brambles.

Doors Lead to Paths

OVER THE INTERVENING TWENTY YEARS, we used that line (see the line from A to F on the map) for the main path and sight line between house and garden (1.1 & 1.2), to draw the two into a marriage as well as generate the position and dimensions of beds throughout the garden. In fact, the lines of every straight bed in our garden are parallel or perpendicular to that line from front door to apple tree that Howard so quietly mentioned.

We tell this story about Howard Andros, who died in 2001 at

1.1 *(previous spread)* MAY *Built in the 1760s, this house and attached barn is at the center of our garden; the front door gave rise to our most important garden path.*

1.2 *(below)* OCTOBER 1, 1983 *Gordon and Nate taking a break from scything brambles and clearing brush under the old apple tree.*

the age of ninety-four, because it sets up the starting point for twenty years of work, passion, and thought about how to design and build a garden. By way of introduction, we want to walk you quickly through the whole garden. Then we'll take more time in subsequent chapters to look at the nature of itinerary and how it can help you design an engaging walk through the gardens around *your* house.

To help us tell our garden's story, we asked Vermont-based photographer Richard W. Brown to visit five times during 2003. With his twenty-year-old Nikon and tripod, which look like old friends, Richard recorded the garden's seasons and moods. He came in mid-May, late June, August, mid-October, and once more after the first snow flew. When he was here in mid-May, he photographed the garden following our itinerary—the path that Mary and I follow virtually every evening of the growing season. This sequential series of pictures provides a clear introduction to the whole garden.

To further orient you along this itinerary, we asked our friend of twenty years, illustrator Elayne Sears, to draw a map of our garden so you could see where you are along the itinerary, and how all the parts fit together.

The Itinerary

To MARK THE GARDEN ENTRANCE, we planted a yew hedge parallel with the front of the house and the driveway. Opposite the door and on the line to the old apple tree, we built stone steps, three in all, leading down between potted tulips and onto the sunny lawn (1.1). The first feature we encounter is the Crab Apple Orchard, an echo of my childhood growing up on an orchard in New Hartford, Connecticut, that my brother, Peter, continues to work. When in the Orchard, we often turn around for a look back to our house. We see the Orchard from our upstairs bedroom windows (page 13), from the single window in Mary's downstairs study, and from a pair of windows in our downstairs sitting room.

As we enter the Brick Walk Garden, we come to a sculpture of Jason from the Greek myth of the Argonauts, a reminder of the three months Mary and I spent on Naxos and Crete on a shoestring just after we were married. This sculpture, atop a finely cast pedestal (1.3), sits at the center of a brick circle (E on map) from which four short brick paths radiate toward the four points of the compass, dividing this square garden into four sections. The north path leads into the garden; the south leads out of the garden and under the branches of the old apple tree. The east and west paths lead to pea-stone walkways down either side. Last year we set black locust logs into the ground without top crosspieces to form a muscular yet open pergola.

Coming out of the pergola, we walk under the old apple tree to look due south into the Woodland Garden (1.4). Its west side (to the right of the apple tree) is bounded by a dirt road; the south side is bounded by an old stone farmer's wall lined with mature black cherry, black locust, and sugar maple trees. Their trunks frame

1.3 MAY *The locust-post pergola, the brick path, and the apple tree combine with the sculpture of Jason to draw guests south into the first garden areas.*

views to the ten-acre meadow that we bought a few years ago.

From under the apple tree, we can walk on a stepping-stone path into the Woodland Garden, where we get a view of the gazebo (1.5), or we can walk through the purple-leaved Beech Tunnel to the gazebo. Built by our friend Roger Kahle eight years ago, the gazebo is a fine sheltered place to sit and take in this corner of the garden. Its stout timbers also frame views in four directions. Looking east is a view through the branches of a maple tree out onto the meadow and the Three Oaks (1.6). We planted those three pin oaks and placed a bench under them about ten years ago as a reminder of the three oaks that still grow today in the village center in Ebrington in the North Cotswold Hills of England, a mile from where Mary grew up.

When we sit on the bench in the gazebo and face north, we look

1.4 MAY *This sculptural seventy-five-year-old apple tree forms the heart of the garden, and reminds us of the Ranney family who planted the MacIntosh tree.*

up the length of the Long Borders (pages 114–15). As we walk north up the lawn path between the borders, we often turn around to look back to the gazebo (pages 110–11). Or we can take a few steps up to a stone-paved sitting area (K on map) we built so we can sit *in* the border (pages 122–23).

We then walk farther north toward the garden shed and come to the shady Rock Garden under mature maples. We often walk onto this stony mound, left from 200 years of farming, to look back down the length of the Long Borders (6.2). The black ceramic sculpture *Hero* looks down on the Dining Area (1.7), with its blue-stone surface and dining table and chairs, where we often have lunch or dinner during warm summer days when the mosquitoes aren't too bad.

Then we walk out of the Dining Area, passing between two cast concrete baskets of fruit and across a free-form lawn we call the Glade, where we have two choices. To the right, stepping-stones lead along the boxwood hedge and into the native wild plum copse that shelters the Spring Garden. From the stepping-stone path we get a lovely view back among the daffodils and Cornell Pink azaleas, the primroses and the lungworts (1.8).

Leaving the Dining Area, we go around the Spring Garden by following a curving lawn path into the four-quadrant Herb Garden (1.9), the most enclosed place on the property to sit and soak up the sun. If you look closely, you'll see that the far gap in the Herb Garden hedge leads to a set of stone steps up onto the shady Rock Garden. We leave the Herb Garden by walking out of the north gate in the *Viburnum prunifolium* hedge and along a lawn path and yew hedge we planted in the spring of 2003 (8.6). This new hedge runs parallel to the one to the left that we planted fifteen years ago, defining a purely rectangular panel of lawn that sweeps the eye north toward the Dell.

The English staddle stone, that mushroom-shaped ornament to the right in 8.7, invites guests to walk into the Spring Garden from the north, whereas the lawn panel and milk cans draw us across the Dell and farther toward the northern end of the garden.

A set of stepping-stones (1.10) rises through ground covers and between antique milk cans onto the Milking Parlor. From that

1.5 MID-MAY *The gazebo, built in the early 1990s, is the first sitting spot along our itinerary.* Phlox divaricata *scents the air around it for two weeks in May.*

raised vantage we look west (1.11) to the Pool Garden (1.12), where a round pool built into the concrete base of an old silo is the focal point for this corner of the property.

A few years ago we hired Dan Snow, dry-stone waller and writer about stone, to create the most recent addition to our garden

1.6 *(above)* MAY ***By removing a few branches from the maple, we opened a view from the gazebo out to the bench under the Three Oaks.***

and the conclusion of our itinerary—the Paddock—just off the north gable end of our house. From a 150-year-old broken-down stone barn foundation, which we bought and had hauled to our place, Dan built a three-sided enclosure; the fourth side is our barn and house. Then we asked a topiary frame maker from California to fashion three sheep to set into the Paddock (1.13). We stuffed the frames of the ewe and her two lambs with sphagnum moss, and now have a reminder of Mary's childhood growing up on a farm near Chipping Campden in Gloucestershire, where her family kept 150 breeding ewes. We walk from the Paddock through the back door of the barn and have come full circle.

Gardens as Mentors

NOW THAT YOU'RE ORIENTED, let's walk back through the whole garden again looking at it through a design lens. By looking at gardens such as ours with specific design elements in mind—the way garden ornaments are placed, how lawn is shaped relative to planting beds, where garden structures or furniture are sited—patterns begin to emerge. Those patterns lead to an understanding of design principles that you can put to work on your own place. Gardens become mentors.

You can review the photos in this chapter right now, before you read another word. Go back through the photographs and look at each with a design element in mind. Look, for example, only at garden ornaments in each image to note where we placed them. Take a second scan at all the photos that show the different paving materials we chose for paths and terraces—which materials we repeated and which we used only once. Look at how we juxtaposed sunny areas and shady areas, and how we used evergreen plants in different ways.

Above all, note that we made an itinerary, a path that we invariably follow. Your garden needs one too, in part because it helps you make decisions about how to use different garden styles, plants, and moods. The itinerary in any garden acts like the main character in a novel; each garden area is a separate chapter in which the main character acts and reacts to differing situations that reveal his or her character. I can assure you that the present clar-

1.7 (overleaf) MAY We work with, not against, nature. Rather than try to garden within the matted roots of a maple/ash copse, we made a shady, stone-paved dining area.

ity of itinerary came only after years of work and thought on how best to link the parts to create a whole, how we'd create continuity, balance, and overlap so that one area would fuse gently with the next.

We designed the garden around an itinerary because it helps answer tough design questions such as "What's next?" By contrasting informal and formal, noisily planted beds and quietly planted ones, sun and shade, extroverted moods and introverted ones, expansive spaces and narrow ones, we knew what to do and what not to do. By making these contrasting elements subtle, we fashioned cohesion between and among all the parts. Here's one design consideration that our itinerary helped with.

1.8 MAY *The curving boxwood hedge (far background) sweeps guests from the Dining Area north toward the Spring Garden.*

1.9 MAY *The Herb Garden is a hedged space unlike any other in our garden. Light-colored, crunchy pea stone gives it even clearer definition.*

Vary Sunlight and Shade

AFTER FOLLOWING OUR GARDEN'S ITINERARY a few years ago, a visitor told us she had felt seven different temperatures. What she noticed is that we have consciously manipulated sun and shade so we experience heat and coolness in varying degrees as we walk along the paths.

When entering the garden just across the driveway from the south door of the house, we are in full sun. As we approach the Orchard, there is a hint of filtered shade, especially under the arching branches of the trees. As we walk into the Brick Walk Garden, full sunlight reasserts itself, only to give way for two or three brief intervals to filtered shade from the moonvine honeysuckle (*Lonicera prolifera*) and *Wisteria* 'Aunt Dee' overhead.

Leaving the Brick Walk Garden, we pass into the deep shade of the apple tree, and it is here that we first feel the temperature drop

two or three degrees. As we walk out from under the apple's branches, we move into full sun for just a moment, then full shade in the purple-leaved Beech Tunnel. We come into full sunlight for a few steps, then back into shade in the gazebo. Sitting on the bench in the gazebo, we look up the Long Borders bathed in full sun. And so it goes, sun to shade to filtered shade to sun to shade. The temperature varies as we walk through our garden, and we respond to it viscerally. We're engaged—if not consciously, at least subconsciously.

Perhaps the warmest part of the garden is the 60-foot-long panel of lawn (B on map) just before the Orchard. The coolest part is in a wedge of constant shade along the north side of the barn and under the branches of the ash, maple, and Japanese tree lilac. Shade in this part of the garden combines with the cooling sound of splashing water in the Pool Garden (W on map).

Structures Vary Light and Shade

STRUCTURES OFFER varying degrees of light and shade, breeze and stillness. Our gazebo is open on all four sides and sits along a line of black locust, black cherry, and maples as well as a nearby *Stewartia pseudocamellia*. During the summer, when the sun is high in the sky, the bench and two chairs in the gazebo are in full shade. The predominant breeze is from the southwest, so we planted shrubs on either side of the gazebo to funnel the breeze through the open south side. Now that the *Magnolia stellata* and *Rhododendron* 'Aglo', planted on the east and west sides, are mature and doing their job, we can sit in the gazebo's cool shade with a nearly constant gentle breeze on our backs. That breeze also keeps mosquitoes at bay most of the growing season. It's a perfect refuge on a hot summer afternoon.

The grape arbor in the Herb Garden works differently. This garden is entirely enclosed, bounded on the north, south, and east by 8-foot-tall hedges and on the west by the garden shed. It is to this enclosure, sheltered from all breezes, that we gravitate in the cooler temperatures of spring, early summer, and fall. The arbor against the east wall of the garden shed is 8 feet tall, and the dense shade cast by the Aurora and Van Buren grapevines keep the sitting space in shadow from noon until sunset. Even so, some

1.10 MAY *We left this one-hundred-year-old milking parlor floor, once within one of the Ranneys' barns, intact. Standing on the concrete floor, looking north, we see their farm.*

sunlight makes its way through the leaves, shedding an appealing dappled shade. To keep the stone paving under the arbor from gathering too much heat during the morning hours, we planted *Thymus minus* in the gaps between the pavers, giving us the feeling of cool, fragrant green underfoot.

This shady grape arbor contrasts with the adjacent Herb Garden, which, as befits herbs, is in full sun from dawn until at least four or five in the afternoon.

1.11 MAY *This area was once covered by two-story barns. The previous owner put up the red-painted boards to close off the remaining barn.*

36

Contrasting Volumes of Space

ONE OF OUR PRIMARY AIMS in our own garden and in those designed for clients is to develop spaces that convey moods and elicit emotion. Over twenty years of trial and error, we find that our garden evokes a range of emotional experiences as we walk from tall to broad, confined to open, sheltering to exposed. Through itinerary, we control the flow of experience so that the emotional message of each area is clear through subtle contrast with areas adjacent to it. The more experiences you provide, the bigger your garden feels.

You create the same emotional variety in your home when you usher visitors from the entry hall to the sitting room and then the kitchen. And why does everyone seem to end up in the kitchen? It's informal, personal, comfortable, lively, lived in, and filled with the good smells of a meal being prepared. Our appreciation of how comfortable the kitchen is becomes crystal clear when we pass from the more formal sitting room to the lively kitchen. Pleasing, subtle contrast is the aim here.

When we walk through the garden entrance, for example, we pass through a narrow gap in a low yew hedge, made narrower by the richly planted pots set on the stone steps. The entrance space then expands into a broad, sunny lawn; the sky is the roof over both the narrow entry and the broad lawn. This area is enclosed on its west side by a lilac hedge and a hundred-year-old maple (D on map), both of which give us privacy from the nearby dirt road. The area to the east is open, offering views into the garden and the meadows beyond.

Then the volumes of space begin to change. Broad lawn gives way to the more confined space where the branches of the crab apple trees hold sway. The sense of being under or among small-scale trees provides a degree of familiarity and comfort, and the shade they offer is welcome on a hot day.

We proceed into a very different space, one commanded by the colonnade of black locust logs. Again, the sky is the roof over this long, narrow, dramatic space. We then broaden the space between the upright logs by creating a wide circle, but as we do, we simultaneously put a roof over our heads in the form of vines held aloft by thick ropes attached to the tops of the locust logs. The feeling in this space is contained but not constrained; we see between and through the locust columns.

From the locust colonnade we walk under the old standard apple tree, whose enormous canopy provides an umbrella of muscular branching and delicate leaves. As we walk out from under the apple's arching branches, the sky again becomes the roof, but only for a moment.

Contrasting Surfaces Underfoot

SIMPLY BY CHANGING paving materials—providing thresholds—we emphasize the transition from one space to another. By limiting ourselves to a few materials, we underpin the coherence of our garden, keeping it from becoming busy. For example, we move across the crushed gravel of our driveway onto mica schist steps that lead into the garden. We then walk across lawn and onto brick as we pass through the locust colonnade. Then we're back onto grass under the apple tree before stepping onto the crunchy pea-stone path through the Beech Tunnel. Then we step back onto grass before arriving at the mica schist steps up to the bluestone/brick terrace at the top of the Long Borders. We consciously limited ourselves to that range of materials throughout the property: crushed gravel, bluestone pavers, brick, mica schist fieldstones, pea stone, and lawn. Repeating these materials achieves coherence while marking transitions.

What's the Big Idea?

BEFORE TAKING A CLOSE LOOK at each of the garden areas along our itinerary, let's go back to the overarching idea—the Big Idea—that generated ideas for all those garden areas. Just as a novelist or a composer needs a theme for a book or a symphony, garden designers need a theme that helps direct decisions about what to do and what not to do.

In a sense, the itinerary of our Vermont garden tells our story as individuals and as a family living in a certain region on a certain property in a certain house. The Big Idea for our garden comes out of the experiences we have shared over twenty-six years, and how

1.12 MAY *We built this pool on the base of a long-abandoned silo near the end of our itinerary.*

our stories are intertwined with the 200-plus-year story of this place. But it took us a while to decide that that was, in fact, what would drive the design of the garden.

When we were taking our first tentative design steps in the mid-1980s, we talked a lot about how we could organize the garden. We considered creating a period garden of the sort the original settlers would have made when they built this house. That would mean rustic fenced areas for fruits and vegetables, a Sturbridge Village–like set of stone walls, perhaps, with a small pond, a cutting garden, and no lawn but plenty of meadows and wildflowers, all of which would express the farm background that Mary and I shared. This broad idea also appealed because it would acknowledge the house and the history of the place. In the end, though, it felt too constricting and a bit precious. Where would Nate play basketball, and where could we play croquet and volleyball? We considered a naturalistic garden, one that flowed and swept and fused with the existing woodland edges, with a bit of lawn here and a lot of lawn there. But we both knew that would not work. We prefer orderly spaces.

After a few more failed attempts at finding the Big Idea, we looked inward at our own experiences and personalities. We three had visited a lot of gardens in England, both traditional and modern, and what appealed to us was the central precept of English garden design: informal planting within firmly structured spaces. Given that Mary is from Old England and I'm from New England, given that I had started my career in gardens, restoring those around the Broadwell Manor House in Gloucestershire, and given that we both liked cleanly organized spaces, but given that we were living in an old farmhouse in Vermont, we thought we would create an Old England–New England hybrid. The primary lines of the garden would be straight and with a certain degree of formality and clarity; the plantings within those beds would be relaxed, and we would leave plenty of lawn for Nate. The background for the beds would be the meadows and fields we see through the mature trees and over the stone walls at the edge of what would become our $1^{1}/_{2}$-acre garden, a boundary we made a pact not to go beyond. Enough is enough.

And so, over the years, we quite naturally began to develop a garden with references to our own lives, while keeping intact those elements of the past that helped us make design decisions. We tried hard to avoid getting designey, self-conscious, and bitty. We tried hard to create a welcoming garden that has naturally grown out of the place and out of us.

1.13 JUNE *We like to offer lots of different yet related experiences as guests walk through our garden. Here is the simplest area of all: a topiary ewe and her two lambs grazing in their paddock.*

2

The Entry Garden,
Sunny Lawn,
and Orchard

WHAT A HOUSE IT WAS that we moved into on December 1, 1983. To heat it I had to light a match to start up a twenty-year-old furnace that was designed to heat a mobile home; after getting my eyebrows singed twice, I pulled the thing out and put in a wood-burning furnace. The windows rattled in the wind, so we taped plastic sheeting over them to keep in some of the heat. We repaired one of the chimneys for the new furnace but could still see between the bricks of the second one. The walls held no insulation, and we had to replace all the wiring and plumbing, and everything in the kitchen and bathroom. Wall lath showed where plaster had fallen. Ragged patches of wallpaper clung to bits of wall. Nate had his fifth birthday party that December in the midst of all this. Throughout that first winter, we scraped wallpaper and sanded every floor in the house. Mary plastered holes in the walls, and Nate and I took down the second chimney so Andre Bernier could rebuild it.

Then it was spring and we were in the garden.

2.1 MAY *Over the last twenty years, we developed these gardens along the visual line to which Howard Andros drew our attention.*

Early Days

YEARS BEFORE we bought what the locals know as the Old Buxton Place, David Reed, its previous owner, had felled, cut, and split into firewood two ancient, diseased sugar maples that had been growing about fifteen feet from each other across the driveway from the front door. He left 3-foot-tall stumps in the ground. When we arrived in 1983, we found that the rotting stumps framed a view from the main door to a rusting yellow Toyota Corolla, dead in the long grass (2.2). The location of those maples, planted in the mid-1800s, clearly related to the front door.

The Entry Garden

ONE OF OUR FIRST IMPROVEMENTS to the entry area was the removal of an unsightly trio: a yellow Toyota Corolla, the nearby hulk of a Volkswagen bus, and a Nash Metropolitan complete with maple sapling growing through it. Then we were ready to garden. First, we built four broad, shallow mica schist fieldstone steps from the driveway grade, down the gentle slope between the maple stumps, and into the garden (2.1). In choosing that flat, textured, readily available gray schist from Goshen, Massachusetts, we introduced a material that we use in the garden to this day whenever we need informal stepping-stone paths or sets of steps. By using mica schist at the entrance, then using it for informal steps here and there throughout the garden, we sound a reassuring note of coherence.

We made that first set of steps 8 feet wide, using the central 4 feet as a walkway and 2 feet on either side as display space for planted pots and garden ornaments. By building steps in that spot, we took advantage of the habit most people have of stopping at a top step and looking straight ahead before proceeding. This top step focused attention onto the distant apple tree.

Having built the steps, we knew we had better do something special with that pair of stumps. By placing broad steps between them, we made them important, and I was not about to get out my chain saw and cut them to the ground. They were an indication of the past of the place. The stump to the east had a hollow core filled with composted wood; its outer perimeter was solid and remains so

2.2 OCTOBER 1983
*We managed to see beyond
the look of the place to its
deep potential.*

today. In February of that year, when we were flying back from a week on Antigua, Mary looked down at a Caribbean island and saw all the growth flowing down the interior and exterior walls of an extinct volcano. She vividly remembers feeling that it was the perfect model for, of all things, the hollowed-out maple stump. Macrocosm to microcosm: Who knows where design ideas come from? That spring we filled the hollow stump with more compost and soil to raise the level 2 feet, then planted a weeping larch (*Larix decidua* 'Pendula') in the base. This small weeping tree now cascades down the sides of the stump and among the *Sedum spurium* 'Dr. John Creech' we planted around the stump and at the base of the evergreens we planted close by (2.3).

The second maple stump had held up better: only the top 2 to 3 inches were rotten. We troweled out a planting pocket in the rotted wood, dug in a mix of topsoil and sand, and planted hens and chicks (*Sempervivum* spp.), which are flourishing there today.

Following the precept of starting small and building on your success, we wanted to expand our bit of a garden, but we didn't want rotted tree stumps to be quite so obvious. Given that Mary sees this entrance to the garden through her study window year-round, we wanted a full range of plants: trees, evergreen and deciduous shrubs, perennials, ornamental grasses, and bulbs.

2.3 LATE OCTOBER *By juxtaposing the shorn yew and the dwarf Scots pine with a deciduous weeping larch, we took advantage of the pleasing contrasts offered by these compatible plants.*

Plant Forms and Foliage Colors

FIRST, WE PLANTED THE PAIR OF UPRIGHT YEWS (*Taxus x media* 'Hicksii'), which today we shear to 3-foot-square, 4-foot-high sentinels to contrast with the informality of the stumps and the mounded form of the single dwarf Scots pine (*Pinus sylvestris* 'Nana') next to it. In juxtaposing these two plants, we introduced foliage contrast as well—the gray-blue needles of the Scots pine against the dark green yew. The weeping larch (*Larix decidua* 'Pendula'), with its striking yellow fall foliage, added another element. In 2003 we planted an upright bloodgood maple (*Acer palmatum* 'Twombly's Red Sentinel'), which nurseryman Ken Twombly from Monroe, Connecticut, had given us. This addition introduced an upright burgundy red to the mix (2.4). We underplanted the gray-foliaged Scots pine with the darker evergreen ground cover

2.4 OCTOBER *Evergreens in the Entry Garden act as a backdrop to the wild colors of annuals in pots; in winter these evergreens become foreground.*

Cliff Green (*Paxistima canbyi*) interplanted with blue oat grass (*Helictotrichon sempervirens* 'Sapphire'). The blue oat grass we added, along with the Cliff Green, brought this otherwise shrubby combination into balance and gave it three levels of interest—evergreen shrubs, deciduous shrubs, and herbaceous ground covers—to complete a set of strong visual contrasts that work well together from the ground up.

Across the steps from this group of shrubs we planted a second yew, which, like its matching pair, we shear into a sentinel. We did not repeat the dwarf Scots pine, because it would have made this grouping too symmetrical and formal. Instead we planted three red-variegated switch grass (*Panicum virgatum* 'Shenandoah'). Each stands out in contrast to its neighbors in different ways throughout the year, and everything stands in balance on either side of the steps.

By using these evergreen and foliage plants rather than complex flowering perennials, we created a background for the plantings of annuals in pots that we change every year (2.5 and 2.11).

Having planted either side of the steps, we knew that to make a true entrance we needed to extend a hedge east and west so guests had no choice but to walk down, not around, the steps. Rather than risk too unsettled a look by introducing yet another species, we planted a yew hedge—fifteen *Taxus* x *media* 'Hicksii'— to the east and west of the steps. The hedge reads as an extension of the two existing sentinel yews on either side of the steps and became a background for beds of herbaceous perennials and evergreen shrubs on their north and south sides.

We knew we wanted to anchor either end of the hedge with something, but only when we got down into the garden and looked back did we realize we needed trees.

By planting trees at either end of the new hedge, we would frame the well-proportioned gable end of the house, visible when looking back from the Brick Walk Garden. We decided that a tall, upright tree wouldn't hide too much of the house and would complement the nearby maple. We looked at the house and its gray clapboards and white trim and decided to plant two Japanese whitespire birches (*Betula platyphylla japonica*) (2.6). They do triple

2.5 *(opposite)* SEPTEMBER *An engaging entry garden has trees, shrubs, perennials, annuals, stone on the ground, and maybe even a garden shed in the background.*

2.6 *(overleaf)* MAY *We planted crab apples and birches in part to set the attached barn into the background, thereby bringing the south gable end of the house into the foreground.*

Seasons in the Entry Garden and Orchard: 1. MAY *A profusion of color, a welcome spring.* 2. SEPTEMBER
Color in annuals lifts the look in early autumn. 3. LATE OCTOBER *The Vermont light and sky set off foliage season.*

4. JANUARY *The winter garden is structured green and black, white and blue.*

duty by framing the handsome gable end of the house, by putting a view of both barn to the east and road to the west into the background, and by strengthening the entrance garden.

As we enter our driveway, the 2-foot-high yew hedge on the right establishes a strong foreground that sets the garden beyond into the background. As we walk down the steps and through the yew hedge, we feel that we are entering a new space. As we look back toward the house, the hedge acts as background for perennials and shrubs. Gardens, especially complex ones, need these simple backgrounds so that color, texture, and foliage stand out.

Separate Garden from Street

NEXT, IT SEEMED CLEAR, we needed to separate the western edge of the garden from nearby McKinnon Road, even though it was dirt and used infrequently. We took stock of what was already growing there; it was just enough to give us the core of an idea. About ten old lilacs were growing under a hundred-year-old maple, the trunk of which was only about ten feet from the edge of the road. Keeping in mind what noted gardener Penelope Hobhouse had once told us, "Whenever in doubt, repeat," we added more lilacs (D on map) along the sunny area where the garden ran up to the road. In that way we made new match old, a device we use time and time again as we develop our garden on this old place. We started by planting five Japanese tree lilacs (*Syringa reticulata*) 18 feet on center, then underplanting them with *Syringa vulgaris* hybrids. We ended up with a tall lilac hedge with staggered bloom periods (the tree lilacs bloom a full ten days or so after the *Syringa vulgaris* hybrids).

The story behind the tree lilacs stretches back to that first visit from Howard Andros in the spring of 1984. When Howard arrived that day, he got out of the car and handed me a coffee can full of compost-enriched topsoil out of which about thirty 1-inch-tall Japanese tree lilac seedlings were popping. Mary and I planted them in a holding bed across the road from the house, and three years later transplanted them as 4-foot saplings. They are now 25 feet tall.

Transcend Foundation Planting

YEARS BEFORE WE BOUGHT OUR HOUSE, someone had built a stone retaining wall about 6 feet out from the south face of the house. The stones, some of which were 6 feet long and 18 inches square, were lined up to create a raised planting bed. Howard came for another spring visit in 1985. This time he gave us a brown paper shopping bag filled with snowdrops (*Galanthus nivalis*) in full bloom, the best time to transplant these spring bulbs. He suggested that we plant half of them along the base of that south-facing stone wall and the other half down in the Woodland Garden, a shadier spot. He pointed out how sun shining on the south side of the wall would heat the stone during the day, warmth that the stone would release into the nearby soil at night, thereby thawing it sooner than the soil elsewhere. Sun and stone together, he said, would create a microclimate that would encourage the snowdrops to bloom well ahead of those planted in the shadier, cooler woodland. In this way we extended the snowdrop bloom in our garden by at least two weeks. Twenty years later we still use this idea when planting bulbs.

There is a second microclimate between the stone retaining wall and the house. Many forces converge to make this south-facing spot hot and dry: the house keeps the north wind at bay all winter; through the stone foundation, the house shares what heat there is in the cellar with that long, narrow strip of garden; sunlight reflects off the light gray walls and white trim of the house; the stone wall gathers heat during the day and releases it at night; and the stone wall is raised, so it drains readily. Hot and dry. Hot and dry. It was a perfect place for a midsummer mass of *Nepeta x faassenii* 'Walker's Low', a catmint in which our little orange puss Ginger loves to sleep (2.7); Russian sage (*Perovskia* 'Longin') for late summer; and a golden-leaved spirea (*Spiraea japonica* 'Goldflame') by the doorway for foliage contrast, among other heat-tolerant perennials and shrubs (2.8).

2.7 *(opposite)* JULY
Ginger asleep in the catmint..

2.8 *(below)* AUGUST
Our dark red front door just 12 feet away inspired this combination of a dark red daylily and the purple-leaved ninebark.

**Persistent Crab
Apple Fruit**

1. OCTOBER
The profuse fruit of
Malus *'Prairiefire'.*

2. FEBRUARY
*The red fruit holds
until April when a flock
of cedar waxwings will
take them in a single
day.*

2.9 *(above)* JUNE *Planted
pots, steps, lawn, more pots,
sentinel yews, and locust logs
all culminate in a sculpture to
draw guests into our garden.*

2.10 *(above)* AUGUST
*The view from our upstairs
bedroom window.*

The Crab Apple Orchard

THE IDEA FOR THE CRAB APPLE ORCHARD was predicated on two things. First, it echoed the orchard I grew up on. Second, we had to find a place for four *Malus* 'Adams' specimens that I ordered for clients who subsequently changed their minds. Was I going to return those beautiful 10-foot-tall crab apples to the nursery in Massachusetts? You know what Benjamin Franklin said: "A tree in the ground is worth two in the nursery." But where were we going to put them?

We considered planting them in two pairs across from one another right in the Long Borders, but that would mean breaking the pattern we had established with red-leaved barberries. We could have put one here and one there, but we had a matched foursome, whose impact would be enhanced by planting them in a row. That's when the orchard idea hit us. But where to put it?

We looked to existing lines of beds for clues. It was soon clear that we'd plant the four crab apples in two beds, two trees per bed, on either side of the main path between the standard apple tree and the front door of the house (2.9). The beds would run east-west, parallel with the straight north edge of the Brick Walk Garden, a line parallel with the gable end of the house and the yew hedge that separated Entry Garden from driveway. Every straight line in our Entry Garden, Orchard, and Brick Walk would be parallel or perpendicular to one another and to the house (2.10). Every bed would line up with the others, thereby creating a rectangular panel of lawn between the line of crab apples and the Entry Garden.

Now the question was, exactly where do we plant the crab apples? This is where we used a remarkably powerful yet simple concept to create visual relationships between the parts of our garden. Arithmetic is at the bottom of it all.

First, we made the east and west ends of the beds line up with the east and west edges of the Brick Walk Garden, so we could set up a visual relationship between existing and new beds (C and E on map). We laid out the Orchard—which now comprises three rows of four crab apple trees—using a module of 2 feet to make decisions regarding the width of the beds under the crab apples as well as the three lawn paths that grow between the rows.

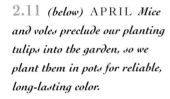

2.11 *(below)* APRIL *Mice and voles preclude our planting tulips into the garden, so we plant them in pots for reliable, long-lasting color.*

We made the beds under the trees 4 feet wide and the east-west lawn paths 6 feet wide. Because we wanted the north-south path to be the dominant one, being the visual link between the south door of the house and the standard apple tree, we increased the width of that path to 8 feet. We planted the trees in each bed 16 feet apart, leaving 4 feet of space between the trees and the ends of the 24-foot-long beds. As the branches of the trees arch over the lawn paths, we'll prune the tips of the arches to 8 feet for easy passage under them.

Once the crab apple orchard was in place, we underplanted the trees with hardy geraniums, an idea that came directly from a visit we made to Jenkyn Place in Hampshire in England many years ago. We were also following another important concept of garden design: theme and variation.

Theme and Variation

ESTABLISHING COHERENCE within each garden area and between those areas is one of the primary tasks of the garden designer. Whether we are designing an entrance garden, an herb garden, a collection of potted plants, or a small perennial garden out back, the touchstone of theme and variation has helped narrow our choices and prevented us from creating a busy-looking garden that is some of this, some of that.

In this example, the theme is an orchard of crab apples underplanted with hardy geraniums; the variation within that theme is in the individual rows of different crab apples and the geraniums we plant under them. Under the first row of four *Malus* 'Adams', with their reddish-pink flowers, we massed *Geranium platypetalum* (2.12), with its electric blue flowers that would bloom ten days or so after the crab apples completed their flowering. Under the second row of four *Malus* 'Sugar Tyme', with their light pink flowers, we planted the pink-flowering *Geranium oxonianum* 'Claridge Druce'. Under the third row of four *Malus* 'Prairiefire', with its white bloom, we interplanted 'Claridge Druce' with the blue-flowering *Geranium pratense* 'Brookside'. The subthemes within this combination are that all crab apples have persistent fruits and all the geraniums have characteristic deeply lobed leaves, yet the crab apples and geraniums have different color flowers.

Two Seasons in the Orchard— Brick Walk

1. MAY *The firm straight lines of lawn paths and brick walkway give structure to a profusion of color, form, and texture.*

2. DECEMBER *A new structure emerges: the lines of crab apples, evergreens, and locust logs focus on the apple tree highlighted in white.*

2.12 JUNE *Planted pots set among flowering perennials in the crab apple orchard create striking color combinations.*

Annuals and Perennials

HAVING UNDERPLANTED THE CRAB APPLES, we added pots to the inner ends of the six beds to draw even more attention to the main north-south path. We bought 20-inch-diameter terracotta pots, set them absolutely level, and filled them with a soilless mix of perlite, vermiculite, fertilizer, and peat using a prepackaged product called Pro-Mix here in the Northeast. Then we filled the pots with bright-flowered plants whose colors would carry the eye from the Entry Garden, across the Sunny Lawn, and through the orchard to the large apple tree, the sculpture of Jason, and the upright posts that framed the entrance to the Brick Walk Garden. If we could draw visitors into the heart of the Brick Walk Garden, they would be firmly launched onto our intentional itinerary. One year we planted pots with two *Argyranthemum* 'Butterfly', with its daisylike bright yellow flowers that last, with some deadheading, throughout the summer. We underplanted them with three *Helichrysum petiolare* 'Limelight', with its bright chartreuse foliage. Then, so as not to become garish, we toned down the yellows with a purple: three per pot of *Heliotropium* 'Fragrant Delight'. When the geraniums are in bloom—they bloom for several weeks—the combination of the annuals in pots and the geraniums in the ground is irresistible (2.13).

The Whole Makes the Parts

COHERENCE—the relationship of the parts to the whole—is one of the most complex concepts to achieve in any garden, no matter what its size. In architect Christopher Alexander's book on form (*The Pattern Language*), he writes that in a coherent design, the parts are not made to create the whole, but the whole creates its parts. This is exactly what has been happening in our garden, and it wasn't until I read Alexander's book in the winter of 2003 that it became clear. This is such a simple yet crucial idea to grasp. Once you do, designing the layout of your garden will be much simpler. Here's an example of what he means.

We did not design the Orchard as a separate element in the overall garden. We didn't create a new episode along the itinerary that somehow magically fit in. We designed the new in relation to the existing whole by lining up the outer ends of the Orchard with the outer edges of the existing Brick Walk Garden; the inner ends lined up with the black locust colonnade down the center of the Brick Walk Garden (page 61). The alignment of the three rows of crab apples then came from the north edge of the Brick Walk Garden, which in turn was parallel with the south gable end of the house 150 feet away. The existing width of the path into the Brick Walk Garden and the gaps between the black locust uprights generated an idea for the width of the lawn paths separating the three rows of crab apples. The sight line down the middle rows of crab apples lined up with the sculpture of the Green Man (more about him later.) We then underpinned that coherence by using lawn—not some new material—to hold these elements together visually.

That is, we designed the Orchard (and every element in our garden) as an extension of existing conditions, terrain, gardens, and features, not as separate episodes that would in some vague way make up part of the whole garden. House, paths, sight lines, materials, plants, framed views, edges, major trees, and existing stone walls—everything relates. No need to complicate your design elements; just follow the obvious visual and spatial clues.

2.13 JUNE *The length of the lawn path between two rows of crab apples leads the eye to a standing stone that marks the base of steps up onto the Rock Garden: part relates to whole.*

3

The Brick Walk Garden and the Apple Tree

ONE DAY IN JUNE 1984 Nate got out his Tonka dump truck, I got out our heavy-duty rototiller, and we made our way over to the abandoned vegetable garden. I started up the rototiller and headed into the area to loosen grass and bramble roots when the motor struggled and stopped. The tines had caught the edge of a nylon rug, the strands of which wrapped around the tines and the axle; David Reed must have used the rugs as mulch years ago. Half an hour later I had the nylon out of the rototiller, but we still had to get the rug up before continuing. It turned out to be more than one rug. The stumps and root systems of maple saplings we had cut down earlier were entangled in nylon; the roots of brambles I had scythed to the ground were growing through the nylon; the roots of quack grass had a firm grip on the nylon. It was one 40-foot-square mess.

In those early days, design issues took a backseat to The Cleanup: rotten barn siding, rusting metal roof panels, and rotten asphalt siding shingles; nails, hinges, old iron wheel frames, the metal remains of a wooden wagon, a 12-foot-long maple sap evaporator pan, tires, wheels, axles, and broken rusted hoes, forks, shovels, and trowels; rotten window frames; broken glass and bottles that, even twenty years later, we're still finding; whole and broken bricks; barbed wire and strands of wire fencing in hun-

dreds of little bits; hundreds of feet of coiled wire just under the surface of the ground; and boards, boards everywhere, with their buried ends rotten. It was a sight.

Farming is not the tidy enterprise that gardening is—being children of farmers, Mary and I knew that—and we were relentlessly headed toward "tidy." We made our way through 200 years of mess knowing what a remarkable place this was under all the junk. In the end, we pulled up the nylon rugs, uprooted the saplings and brambles, transplanted our daylilies and peonies, and made our first inroads toward a garden. Notwithstanding that when my mother first saw the property she burst into tears, we knew we had a gem of a place, and a couple of years later she did too. The problems were all on the surface; underneath this neglected exterior, the structure of the house was sound, the topsoil a foot thick.

When we launched into making the Brick Walk Garden, we had precious few clues from The Whole to help us. There were the remnants of the vaguely rectangular vegetable garden punctuated with the nylon-rug-plagued thorny brambles and tenacious quack grass. We had previously removed the maple saplings and opened up some ground for a few carloads of transplants we brought from our previous garden just 8 miles away, but other than that, the possibilities were wide open.

Starting a Design

WE STRUGGLED WITH THE DESIGN of the Brick Walk Garden for years. We could not get it right. With the help of young David Marx, then an employee of my garden installation business, we laid down the straight brick path on line with the side door of the house and the standard apple tree. The path would be the spine of a roughly square garden 60 feet on each side. But as we were laying the path, we got cute. Instead of running it straight all the way through the center of the garden, we laid a circular path in the middle of the garden that ran around the edge of an 18-foot-diameter circular planting bed. For some unknown reason, we massed the ornamental grass *Panicum virgatum* in that circle. It looked awful.

We took out the grass months later and put in a combination of

3.1 *(previous spread)* JUNE *Our imaginations are engaged when we walk into, not by, a garden. And once within a profuse garden, we delight in a strong visual center—in this case, the brick circle and the sculpture—that our eye can go out from and return to.*

The Path West of the Brick Walk

1. SUMMER 1990 *The lawn path received sufficient sun for several years, but trees and shrubs grew and shaded the area.*

2. JUNE 2002 *We took the shaded lawn up and put pea stone down, providing a warm, dry place for our cat Onza to nap.*

Two Seasons in the Brick Walk

1. JUNE *Peony 'Claudia' marks the entrance. Claudia was the daughter of Professor A. P. Saunders (1869–1953), who was an important peony hybridizer in New York State and a friend of Howard Andros.*

2. JANUARY *Vermont's winter lasts from early November until late March. We pay attention to that fact when we choose places for materials, evergreens, and garden ornaments and when we prune important trees.*

boulders and alpines. They looked dreadful. A year later we laid stone to mark the four points of the compass in the circle. No better. After three years of experimenting, we gave up and paved the whole circle with matching brick. That looked great. By having brick on the ground rather than plants, we opened up the view all the way from the front door to the apple tree trunk, a view that we had lost sight of with the grasses and all those other foolish installations.

What we had left were two 60-foot-long beds, each about 28 feet wide with a brick circle in the middle. We tried one combination of shrubs and perennials after another; nothing looked good. What was the problem? The path gave us little clue as to what to do. All the focus was on the line between the apple tree and the Entry Garden, and these two badly proportioned beds were just

3.2 JUNE We combine big plants with contrasting bold foliage such as Aruncus dioicus, Hosta 'Sagae', and Cimicifuga ramosa 'Atropurpurea' in the 60-foot-square Brick Walk and then anchor those herbaceous plantings with the upright evergreen arborvitae (Thuja occidentalis 'Smaragd').

along the side of this central axis. There was little or no engagement between path and beds.

Then one day it hit us. We would add two east-west paths on line with the center of the brick circle (3.1). That would divide these two long, ungainly gardens into four parts. Once we installed the new cross paths, we had a four-quadrant garden with a brick circle in the center. It looked much better. What we had done was divide two unmanageable spaces into four manageable ones, a gesture that eased both design and maintenance. Design ideas began to flow for the first time.

Mark Centers

GIVEN THAT WE WANTED to draw people into the heart of this area, we decided to mark the center of the brick circle by placing a sculpture there that could be seen from the Entry Garden. One day we happened upon Jerry and Gloria Levine's Hayloft Art Gallery, near Mount Snow, and found a modestly priced 18-inch-high plaster vase in the form of the head of Jason from the Argonauts. We bought it instantly. We placed our previously purchased refined English cast stone pedestal in the center of the brick circle and set Jason atop it facing the Entry Garden (page 70). Being such a handsome sculpture set on a fine pedestal, Jason provides the garden with the crucial center it had lacked for years.

As successful as the cross paths were, especially with Jason installed, things were still not right, but we couldn't define the problem. In June 1987, in the midst of our struggles, Mary and I traveled with clients Peter and Theodora Berg to southern England to look at houses and gardens designed by architect Sir Edwin Lutyens. Peter had read widely on Lutyens's work and wanted to see some of it firsthand; we also wanted to gain inspiration for the gardens we were working on together at their new home on a mountaintop in southern New Hampshire. We stayed at Little Thakeham, a hotel originally designed by Lutyens as a private home surrounded by formal gardens, near Storrington in West Sussex, southwest of London.

Shortly after settling into our room at Little Thakeham, Mary and I met Theodora in the garden for a walk. We came down a set

3.3 JUNE *We chose black locust posts for the colonnade in part to echo the indigenous black locusts in the background, linking cultivated garden to existing landscape.*

of steps directly off the back doors of the house, and there was a beautiful pergola. Roses festooned the oak crosspieces, which were supported by brick pillars. That was it. We would build a pergola down both sides of all four paths and the central circle of our Brick Walk Garden. But given that our garden was adjacent to a 200-plus-year-old farmhouse in southern Vermont and not a highly refined Lutyens house in England, we'd design a pergola to meet our own needs.

Materials Echo Nature

WHEN WE RETURNED HOME, we looked to existing features and to the nature of our developing garden for inspiration for the materials and design for our pergola. Then we spotted it: a dead black locust tree in the hedgerow of the 2½-acre field across the road we had recently purchased from neighbors. We knew that black locust had been used for generations to build long-lasting split-rail fences throughout the Northeast. We also knew that the east end of our 200-year-old barn had been supported from the day it was built with black locust logs buried several feet into the ground; those 24-inch-diameter posts were still so solid we couldn't drive a nail into the wood. As our friend and stone mason Andre Bernier had told us, "Black locust in the ground lasts one day longer than a rock."

We asked logger Calvin Powling to provide about forty 10-foot-long black locust logs, and requested that he be careful not to damage the deeply fissured bark. Calvin also provided us with smaller diameter wood for the crosspieces. We dug holes and set the logs upright. But when we stood back, we realized that once the crosspieces were installed, the whole pergola would look too heavy and massive. We left out the crosspieces, and that's how our colonnade of black locust logs was formed (page 70). We then planted two *Wisteria* 'Aunt Dee' and one moonvine honeysuckle (*Lonicera prolifera*) at the inside base of three of the logs. When the vines needed support above, we affixed 1½-inch-thick hawserlike ropes between the tops of the logs.

The structure of the garden was confirmed the day those upright posts went in. Pairs of posts framed views into other parts

3.4 AUGUST *Pleasing foliage contrast is an essential design principle. Here a sedum, miscanthus grass and dwarf Scots pine complement each other in our autumn garden.*

Three Seasons in the Brick Walk: 1. SUMMER *The strong forms of the* Chamaecyparis *and* Berberis *'Kobold' hedges anchor a profusion of perennials.* 2. AUTUMN *Foliage contrast takes on new meaning in the fall.*

of the garden looking east and west. Along the length of the pergola, the uprights framed views north to the front door of the house and south to the trunk of the old apple tree (3.6). We could also see the posts from many parts of the garden, framing views into the garden from the outside.

Other more subtle things happened with these posts. By clearing some of the lower branches of a black locust (*Robinia pseudoacacia*) growing at the edge of the nearby Woodland Garden, we created a visual link between the Woodland Garden and the Brick Walk Garden (3.3), a subtle echo and an element of coherence between garden and the natural world around it. The locust posts also gave us the idea to plant a hybrid of *Robinia pseudoacacia*—that is, the yellow-leaved *Robinia pseudoacacia* 'Frisia', a tree that we didn't know at the time would become the central plant in our garden at our cottage in England.

3. WINTER *Evergreens, locust posts, and dried ornamental grasses come to the fore against the snow and the tracery of deciduous tree limbs in the background.*

Structural Plants

THE CROSS PATHS, the upright locust logs, the central sculpture, and the four outer edges established the built structure of the garden. And by paving the central circle with brick, we had simplified the garden's core. Now we had to build complex gardens around that simple center.

When choosing plants for a garden area, we followed the classic order of primary, secondary, tertiary. Small trees as well as evergreen and deciduous shrubs formed the primary level; smaller shrubs and major herbaceous perennials formed the secondary level; specimen or massed perennials formed the tertiary level.

We started with the primary level, and looked to the four-quadrant nature of the garden for help. First, we planted an emerald green arborvitae (*Thuja occidentalis* 'Smaragd') near the center of each quadrant to accent the four parts and provide that same structure in winter. We then planted a dwarf Scots pine (*Pinus sylvestris*

'Nana') in the northwest corner of the garden to echo the same plant in the Entry Garden. Two years later we planted a dwarf white pine (*Pinus strobus* 'Nana') in the southeast corner of the garden, not so much for balance as for foliage contrast with the deciduous shrubs and perennials we planted near it.

Plants Choose Their Neighbors

WITH THE EVERGREEN SHRUBS—the core of our winter garden in this area—in place, we chose deciduous shrubs to put next to them to provide pleasing contrasts. (One plant choice helps us make the next.) A purple-leaved sand cherry (*Prunus* x *cistena*) now grows next to one arborvitae, and two gray-blue-foliaged *Rosa glauca* grow next to two other arborvitae. To avoid symmetry in this informally planted garden, we chose a variegated Tartarian dogwood (*Cornus alba* 'Elegantissima') so its light yellow variegation would shine in contrast to the evergreen foliage of an arborvitae during the growing season, and its bright red twigs would glow against that same evergreen foliage in winter.

Once the evergreen and deciduous shrubs were in, they helped us choose herbaceous plants to put next to them for further contrast in foliage, color, flower, texture, or form. *Astilbe japonica* 'Red Sentinel' now grows under the variegated dogwood. *Hylotelephium spectabile* 'Brilliant' contrasts with both the dwarf white pine and the maiden grass (3.4). A sweep of seven sneezeweed (*Helenium* 'Riverton Beauty') grow in front of three switch grass (*Panicum virgatum* 'Heavy Metal'), in part because they bloom simultaneously.

We mass perennials to give the garden drama or a punch of color when and where we need it. We set out large specimens of goatsbeard (*Aruncus dioicus*) in the shadier west quadrants and the purple reed grass (*Miscanthus sinensis* 'Purpurascens') in two of the remaining quadrants. We repeat massed Shasta daisy (*Leucanthemum* x *superbum* 'Becky') here, hollyhocks there (3.5). We set out seven highly fragrant purple-leaved snakeroot (*Cimicifuga ramosa* 'Brunette') in the southwest shady corner to contrast with the yellow-leaved locust. We planted a single *Hypericum frondosum* for its profusion of yellow flowers in August.

Now that we had a structure established by path, pergola, brick

3.5 JULY *For a few weeks, the Brick Walk echoes the English cottage garden of Mary's childhood: hollyhocks, coneflowers, daylilies, delphiniums, among others.*

circle, and Jason, now that we had strong structure in evergreen and deciduous shrubs and large-scale perennials, we planted to our heart's delight, knowing that smaller detail plants had an appropriate context within this structure. Specimen daylilies, bearded and Siberian iris, Oriental poppies, and phlox, among many others, as well as annuals such as *Nicotiana* 'Fragrant Cloud', and perilla, with its deep red contrasting foliage, went in.

Just for the fun of it, we planted a silver willow (*Salix alba sericea*) that Joe Eck and Wayne Winterrowd, fellow gardeners in southern Vermont, had given us. We let it grow for four years, then pollarded it—that is, we cut off the 5-inch-thick trunk 8 feet above the ground in late March and let all the buds break so that in one season these young branches would form a 6-foot-diameter silver globe on an 8-foot-tall trunk there in the northwest quadrant.

3.6 JULY *When guests new to our garden leave the Brick Walk, they are under the apple tree, where they see the roof of the gazebo and know exactly where to go next.*

Contrast Plants with Materials

AFTER PUTTING IN THE CROSS PATHS, it became abundantly clear that they had to lead to something. That something turned first into two lawn paths running down the east and west edges of the Brick Walk Garden (E on map), but lawn seemed like a weak and insufficient destination. To give the east path more visual presence, we planted a dwarf barberry hedge (*Berberis thunbergii* 'Kobold') along the east side of the garden (pages 76–77). For years that 18-inch-high hedge grew between the lawn path and the plantings along the east edge of the Brick Walk Garden. But as time passed and the nearby plants grew, more and more shade was thrown onto this path, making the grass look increasingly ragged.

In 2001, we took up the lawn path and laid down $^3/_8$-inch gray pea stone instead. Instantly the hedge took on new clarity because of the contrasting colors of hedge and pea stone. Given that success, we did the same thing to the lawn path leading down the west side of the Brick Walk Garden that separated it from the adjacent Woodland Garden. You can see for yourself on page 69 what a difference the light-colored stone makes to this shady area of the garden.

Define Depth and Distance

STANDING AT THE TOP OF THAT WEST PATH looking south down its length, we realized that without some object of known size at the far end of the path, where it curved left to lead under the old apple tree, there was little to help people sense distance as they stood at the beginning of the path. They could see hostas and ferns, but how big is a hosta, how big is a fern? We had just purchased two 40-inch-high Colombian urns, and we thought they might help visitors better understand this part of our garden.

Rather than set the pair of terra-cotta urns across from each other at the beginning of the path, which is what we often do with a pair of ornaments, we set one to the right of the beginning of a path and placed the second in the hosta/fern bed where the path curved left, in line with the center of the path (page 69). Now, anyone looking down the path can instantly gauge distance by subconsciously comparing the size of the nearby urn with that of the distant one to gain a clearer understanding of the length of the path and thereby the dimensions of the garden. This is an easy device; we have used pairs of pots, urns, garden sculptures, furniture, even similarly shaped boxwood, yews, or other topiary to help define depth and gauge distance.

Link New Areas to Those Nearby

Now THAT WE WERE INTO THE HEART OF THE GARDEN, we needed to establish links to adjacent gardens in a variety of subtle, honest ways that would not draw undue attention to themselves. Such visual and physical links would ensure that this garden area fit within a coherent plan, albeit one that took us twenty years to develop.

- We repeated the pair of yew sentinels by the entry steps at the north entry to the Brick Walk Garden (page 88: 1, 2) as well as at its south exit.
- We planted a refined Korean maple (*Acer pseudosieboldiana*) across the pea-stone path from the west end of the cross path so it would be framed by the locust post uprights, linking Brick Walk Garden to Woodland Garden.
- By aligning the locust posts with the old apple tree and the front door, we framed views north to the house and Entry Garden (page 88: 3, 4) and south to the apple tree.
- We planted a variegated dogwood at the south end of the Brick Walk Garden, then planted a similarly variegated hosta in the Woodland Garden to the south. We also planted the chartreuse-leaved *Hosta* 'Sunpower' under the dogwood, then repeated the chartreuse foliage in *Hosta* 'Sum and Substance' at the edge of the Woodland Garden.

Use Indigenous Materials

ALTHOUGH WE CREATE these immediate references through framing, color, and plant choice to link nearby garden areas to the Brick Walk Garden—something you will see we did throughout the garden—we also repeat the use of the black locust log throughout the garden. One result of this repetition is coherence; another is the reassuring, quiet use of an indigenous material to link

3.7 (above) MAY *The purple-leaved beech tunnel leads inexorably to the gazebo, and provides a transition between two lawn areas.*

3.8 (overleaf) MAY *Careful pruning turns trunk and branching into sculpture through which distant views are framed.*

the garden to the natural world. As you walk through the rest of the garden with us, you'll see examples of how we used black locust logs and trees as a repeated form. Here is a quick summary:

- posts used to mark entryways through hedges
- gateposts
- shallow steps (set horizontally)
- vine support (Cut off a living black locust tree 18 feet above the ground, and use the remaining post as the support.)
- living link between garden and native woodland (left to grow in the Woodland Garden)

Tree Drip Lines Suggest Edges

ARLY IN THE MAKING OF OUR GARDEN, we were looking at the apple tree growing roughly in the center of what was an arbitrarily shaped curvy patch of lawn with beds planted around its perimeter. There was no relationship between the circular form of the tree, the curvy edge where lawn met bed, and the straight south edge of the Brick Walk Garden.

In trying to determine how to better shape that lawn, we looked to adjacent gardens and the apple tree for clues. The shape of that lawn could help establish a visual link between the Brick Walk Garden, the Woodland Garden, and the western edge of the Long Borders. After considering a number of shapes, none of which were suggested by existing features of the garden, we looked up to see that the circular outline of the apple tree could be repeated on the ground in a circular panel of lawn. The tree had a 30-foot

3.9 JULY *We used the ancient design principle of the circle in the square for the organization of the Brick Walk: the whole garden is square; the brick circle lies at its center.*

86

radius. We loosely tied one end of a 60-foot rope to the base of the tree; then, holding the rope's far end, walked around the perimeter of the lawn. After trying a variety of radii, we settled on a 40-foot radius, because it would enable me to remove as little lawn as possible yet still make 300 degrees of a circle (F on map). The remaining 60 degrees would be squared off at the north edge, where circular lawn met the straight south edge of the Brick Walk Garden.

We had to adjust for major existing features, but by using radii, we created a shape that drew all parts into a sound relationship with one another as they gathered around the circle. (We did the same in our tiny garden in England, as you'll see in Chapter 10.)

I marked the circumference of the circle with thirty or so bamboo stakes, cut the edge with the straight-nosed spade, then lifted the excess sod. By planting new perennials and transplanting others into the newly opened spaces, the edges of adjacent beds took on cleaner, simpler lines: convex fit into concave, and this major lawn circle set up a visual relationship between tree, lawn, and adjacent beds.

Make the Most of Transitions

ONE PROBLEM REMAINED: the 10-foot-wide strip of lawn that linked this new big circle to the area by the gazebo and the bottom of the Long Borders. By leaving this link as lawn, we were not taking advantage of this point of transition. The quiet mood and design of the big circle melted and swept down that 10-foot-wide strip and diluted the drama of the area in front of the gazebo. By taking up that lawn and marking that transition with an arbor or a gate, for example, we could create drama, surprise, and a strong feeling of leaving one space and entering another.

Mary and I thought about gardens we had visited, and recalled a remarkable living hornbeam tunnel we had walked through many times at the Hidcote Manor Gardens, just across the fields from Hidcote Boyce, where Mary grew up. We thought it would be fun to plant some kind of living tunnel to replace this 10-foot-wide, 20-foot-long strip of sloping lawn. We took up the lawn, put down pea stone, and planted five pairs of black haw (*Viburnum*

3.10 JUNE *The trunk of this Zone 3* Wisteria *'Aunt Dee' grew around a locust post for years until we removed the post to show this braided effect.*

Seasons in the Brick Walk: 1. SUMMER *Looking south into the garden.*
2. WINTER *Looking south.*

3. SPRING *Looking north toward the house.*
4. SUMMER *Looking north.*

lentago) to form the tunnel. Unfortunately, they proved to be far too unruly and unwilling to retain the shape of a tunnel. After four years of unsatisfying shearing, we uprooted the lot, in part thanks to Nan Sinton from *Horticulture* magazine.

Nan, our mutual friend Gary Koller (a plantsman and designer), and I were leading a group of twenty or so people through our garden, and when we got to the tunnel, I started grousing about the intractable black haw. Nan suggested we use purple-leaved European beech (*Fagus sylvatica* 'Purpurea') instead. I didn't think it was hardy enough, but Dennis Mareb, a nursery-man in Stockbridge, Massachusetts, said he could supply ten 8-foot-high saplings that had been grown from seed, which would make them much hardier than grafted trees.

We took up the black haws, then made steps down the gentle slope by setting five 8-foot-long black locust logs horizontally to form 3-inch risers, with pea stone between them as the surface on which to walk. I drilled $^3/_4$-inch holes vertically into the ends of the logs, then slipped one end of an 18-foot-long piece of $^3/_4$-inch steel reinforcing rod into the hole on one end of the log and arched the rod over to fit into the hole on the other end, creating metal arches on which to train the beeches. After running and wiring three long pieces of rebar horizontally to link the five arches, we planted five pairs of 8-foot purple-leaved European beech saplings, one at each end of the five locust steps (3.8). When walking from the lawn under the old apple tree toward the gazebo, the tunnel now frames its entrance, turning an indistinct area into a dramatic and hand-some transition.

4

The Woodland Garden

WHEN IT CAME TIME to decide how to garden under the existing maples, locusts, and black cherries at the bottom of the garden, an obvious choice was a woodland garden—that is, a path that wound among understory trees, shrubs, and perennials.

As with all gardens, the first thing we did was to establish the edges, clarifying the limits of our design challenge. The west side of the property is bounded by McKinnon Road, so it became clear that we had to separate road from garden. Without making other planting decisions, we massed shade-tolerant shrubs such as *Hydrangea paniculata* 'Unique', *Viburnum lantana* 'Mohican', and, just last year, leatherleaf viburnum (*Viburnum rhytidophyllum*) along the western length of the Woodland Garden (G on map). Because we rarely visit the Woodland Garden in winter, we didn't include any needled or broad-leaved evergreens in this shrub screen.

The south boundary of the woodland was already established by the stone wall that separates this area from the adjacent 10-acre meadow we purchased in the early 1990s. We removed all the saplings and brush from that southern area of the original property, leaving only major trees to provide shade for the Woodland Garden. The gazebo established the east edge of the Woodland Garden; the Beech Tunnel and circular lawn under the old apple tree established its northern edge. Clearly understanding the edges helped us design the garden within those borders. But before deciding where to place paths and plants, we had to decide which trees to leave and which to remove.

4.1 OCTOBER *The autumn garden aglow with a range of foliage colors and textures in indigenous as well as garden plants.*

Judicious Subtraction

WE WALKED THROUGH OUR BIT OF WOODLAND with bright pink forester's tape to mark trees and shrubs for removal. We tied tape around the trunk of a deeply diseased 175-year-old elm but decided to leave a 6-foot-high stump; after all, this grand master had probably been planted by the people who built the house in the 1760s. (A year later, I planted a division of a climbing euonymus vine next to that stump. The division came from a vine that had been growing at the farm where I grew up; I remembered my father telling me that it in turn had come from a division from the vine growing in his mother's garden on Long Island.)

We also flagged butternut trees; because they were brittle, they would be forever dropping branches and nuts onto any garden we made in this area. We tried to save an ailing apple tree but a few years later accepted that it was too far gone and removed it. We dropped several diseased ash trees but kept a few that were still fighting off the virus attacking ash trees in the Northeast. We also removed countless maple saplings, and several black cherry trees, which attract webworms. After cutting down all these, we sorted out the felled wood.

We had barely two nickels to rub together that first and second winter, because the restoration of the house was demanding every cent we could spare, so we stored the suitable logs for firewood. We needed ten cords of wood to heat our drafty farmhouse; a cord is a stack 4 feet high and wide and 8 feet long. Ten of those stacks every year is a lot of wood. That first winter, we burned all the brush and rotten wood from the felled trees as well as the decaying boards we had unearthed.

One day when Nate and I were tending twelve piles of burning wood, the Ranneys next door thought the place was on fire, and in a sense it was. Having removed the flagged trees, saplings, and brush, we cleared the way to make decisions on the design of the area based on which trees remained (4.1).

We left largely intact a thick, dark copse of tall, narrow, spiny black-stemmed trees that looked like pear. In the early 1900s, the farmers who worked this land must have planted a pear tree in the midst of what is now our Woodland Garden. Early in the development of this area, we discovered the stump of that pear tree surrounded by shoots that had come up from its root system.

4.2 (opposite) AUGUST *Big-leaved hostas look best when planted individually and then surrounded by finer-foliaged plants.*

4.3 (below) OCTOBER *The striking fall foliage of* Fothergilla gardenii *lights up shady areas.*

When Roger Swain (longtime science editor at *Horticulture* magazine and host of the television show *People, Places & Plants*) and his wife, Elisabeth, were in the garden a few years ago, we showed him the stump and copse and asked what he thought the 3- to 4-inch-diameter shoots were. He said that in the late 1800s and into the 1900s, named pear scions such as Bartlett and Anjou were grafted onto indigenous pear rootstock such as *Pyrus ussuriensis*, much as they are today. He thought that this copse of 20- to 25-foot-tall spiny pear trees with their shiny leaves and gnarly fruit were shoots coming up from this original rootstock.

Seeing the potential for an unusual copse, unlike any other in our garden, I pruned the vertical saplings so all their branches are now at least 10 feet above the ground, creating a canopy over the thirty or so stems. This 30-foot-diameter copse with 3-inch-long spines on the

4.4 EARLY MAY 1980S
Before the mice and voles found our new garden, we planted tulips to coincide with the flush of bloom in woodland phlox.

4.5 LATE APRIL Fritillaria
meleagris *blooms with early
daffodils.*

upper branches lent a somber mood to what was otherwise a bright and cheery place under the mature maples, locusts, and black cherries. To me, this corner keeps the Woodland Garden honest (4.8).

The drip line of the copse—that is, the line we could draw on the ground under the outer tips of the branches—gave us a logical place for the outer edge of the Woodland Garden, where the circular lawn under the old apple tree met the edge of the garden. We later underplanted these spiny pears with a variety of dry-shade-tolerant herbaceous plants: *Phlox stolonifera*, *Phlox divaricata*, *Waldsteinia ternata*, *Ajuga reptans* 'Gaiety' and 'Caitlin's Giant', as well as the woody *Stephanandra incisa* 'Crispa', which thrives in deep shade.

Pruning for Aesthetics

AS FOR THE TREES WE SPARED, we pruned them to frame or screen views. Given the beauty of the adjacent meadow to the south, we pruned the lower branches off all the trees (called "limbing up") from the west end of the stone wall to the gazebo. Because we wanted to open views and let sunlight into this dry-shade garden, we pruned all the lower branches up 20 feet or so above ground level. The grand trunks of the remaining trees framed views out into the meadow (4.2).

We also paid attention to one particularly beautiful maple at the east end of the row of trees that was some 30 feet from a fine old black locust. After removing the brush between these two trees, we could see that their trunks framed a view south toward Brattleboro. The spot between those venerable trees became a good place for a bench. To screen a view of our neighbor's house, albeit almost a quarter mile away, we left the lower branches on the maple and a few other trees to the east of that potential sitting area.

The Woodland Garden's Structure

NOW THAT WE HAD CLEARED the woodland of unwanted plants, now that we had limbed up some trees and left lower branches on others, and now that we had established the edges of the Woodland Garden, we began designing the area. We always start with paths. They furnish the internal structure of a garden, and they draw us into rather than around a garden.

Within that dogleg sliver of land existing points of interest helped us determine where to run the paths: the magnificent remaining trees; views through them south into the meadow; wooded ridges fading into the distance; the spiny pear copse.

We wanted to vary the experience of changing light and space as much as possible while also juxtaposing a broad area in full shade with an enclosed area in a pool of sunlight. One moment we wanted to be behind shrubs (4.2) and another in front of an expansive view.

Then there was the ever-changing woodland across the seasons and the sounds associated with them: robins arriving in spring and perching in the topmost branches above a carpet of spring ephemerals; the high-pitched whine in late July of cicadas hiding in the deeply fissured bark of the cherries and locusts and above blooming astilbes and hostas; the piercing call of bluejays in October high among the blazing orange leaves of the maples (4.1).

Link Adjacent Gardens

WE WANTED TO DESIGN woodland paths for this variety of experience, but we also needed to design paths relating to existing garden areas and *their* paths. Three garden areas adjoin the Woodland Garden: the Brick Walk Garden, the lawn area under the old apple tree, and the bottom of the Long Borders. We wanted to link all three (G on map).

The first path to work off of was the pea-stone path that ran between the west side of the Brick Walk Garden and the Woodland Garden. At the south end of that path, right by the Colombian urn, we turn left to walk under the apple tree and toward the Beech Tunnel. Why not start a second path to the right of the Colombian urn that enables us to walk on a dogleg-shaped bark mulch path through the spiny pear copse and down the full length of this garden area before turning east to join another path?

We stood under the apple tree and saw a perfect opening for the beginning of a second path—this one made of stepping-stones—that would lead into the heart of the Woodland Garden (page 101). But where would it come out? The space between the east end of the tunnel and the gazebo was the obvious choice; an

4.6 (opposite) JULY
Astilbes and hostas are a deservedly classic combination for a woodland garden.

4.7 (overleaf) EARLY MAY
Rhododendron *'Aglo'*, Phlox divaricata, Phlox stolonifera *in variety, and the acid green of* Euphorbia polychroma *combine to light up the woodland for two weeks in May.*

entrance there would form yet another part of a seamless itinerary (area between H and I on map) by leading from one path to the next. We installed a stepping-stone path that arced through the woodland, then joined the bark mulch path.

Mark Beginnings

ONE OF THE PROBLEMS that arises with stepping-stone and bark mulch paths is that, at their best, they are well integrated at ground level into the ground covers and plants through which they pass. They're tough to see from a distance. We solved this problem by placing vertical elements at the beginning of these paths. The terra-cotta urn draws guests to the beginning of the bark mulch path. A pair of old granite fence posts we found on the place went on either side of the first stepping-stone near the apple tree (page 101); we set a single granite fence post at the other end of the path, near the gazebo. All these vertical elements drew attention to the beginning of the paths, ensuring their use.

Vertical Elements Structure Horizontal Gardens

STILL THE DRY-SHADE GARDEN lacked structure, especially when not in bloom. During the cleanup of our place, we found nine granite fence posts, some buried under a few inches of leaves or under a rotten barn roof. We set the posts irregularly along the length of the 150-foot-long, 30-foot-wide Woodland Garden (4.7) to mimic an old fence that might have existed decades ago on the farm. These upright stones created a vertical leitmotif, a repeated form that helped hold the garden together visually and add just a bit of drama.

One of the standing stones we set in the garden is quite broad and comes to a point (4.2). Just after we set it in place back in 1986, before the garden grew up to obscure our view of it from the bedroom window, Mary remembers looking out that window at dawn and seeing the light shining off its surface, looking for all the world like a Celtic monument.

I knew that those heavy, cumbersome 6-foot-long slabs of granite were no picnic to set 2 feet or more into the rooty soil of the woodland, so I called a friend, Dan Noss, for some help. He brought his small Kubota tractor with a backhoe one day in the fall of 1986.

Seasons in the Woodland

1. APRIL 1985 *The bones of the Woodland Garden are in place; we had just planted shrubs and perennials.*

2. EARLY MAY 2003 *Our more mature Woodland Garden with* Stewartia pseudocamellia *to the left.*

We worked for the better part of the day digging holes, lowering the stones with straps into place, and backfilling. As Dan was packing up his tractor, we looked back to admire our day's work and he said, "Well, that should about finish your garden, huh?"

A Dry-Shade Garden

NOW THAT WE HAD THE VIEWS OPENED, houses and road screened, edges established, and paths in, now that we had mature trees providing shade, and openings between them allowing sunny spots, we were ready to start planting. Dry shade was what we had to work with, a fact that drove virtually every plant selection we made. Plant choice was also driven by the fact that the bulk of shade-tolerant plants bloom in spring. So we focused on spring-blooming perennials and shrubs, and on foliage and flower color to carry us through the balance of the growing season.

Therein began, sometime in the spring of 1987, a process of trial and error to choose as wide and as hardy and beautiful a set of plants as we can set out in this soil laced with the aggressive roots of maples. We continue to remove some maples in the Woodland Garden as the years go by, but maple trees are so deeply associated with a Vermont garden that we just have to keep the more beautiful specimens, no matter how difficult they are to garden under.

We started our plant choices with shrubs and understory trees. At a lecture in Portland, Oregon, one winter, I saw a slide of *Stewartia pseudocamellia* from Gossler's Nursery, a superior West Coast source of refined trees and shrubs, and I knew we had to have at least two in our Woodland Garden. I ordered them that evening but did not make it clear to Roger Gossler that our Vermont winters were much longer than his in Oregon. That March 15, when we still had 18 inches of snow on the ground, and subzero temperatures regularly, a knock came at the door. It was the UPS deliveryman with a 6-foot-long waxed box from Gossler's. In it were two lovely 6-foot bare-root *Stewartia pseudo-camellia* in full leaf.

We potted them up and kept them in the cold part of our cellar, bringing them into sunlight as often as outdoor temperatures would allow. After a month of coddling these beautiful little trees,

4.8 WINTER *This copse with its dramatic black trunks was in place when we arrived in 1983. All we have done is prune the trees so that their lowest branches are 12 feet or so above the ground.*

we planted them at the beginning and end of the stepping-stone path in the Woodland Garden. Now, nearly twenty years later, they are gorgeous 18-foot-high trees that throw camellia-like flowers in early July. Not far from the *Stewartia*, we set out a *Magnolia* x *soulangiana*, another understory tree.

We also planted groups of shrubs: *Rhododendron* 'Aglo', with its shocking pink flowers in May; the native arrowwood (*Viburnum dentatum*); witch hazel (*Hamamelis virginiana*), for its fall foliage; *Fothergilla gardenii*; and, just this past fall, *Hydrangea arborescens* 'White Dome', a shrub that Connecticut-based nurseryman Ken Twombly gave us.

Once we had these and many other trees and shrubs in, we began planting perennials and ground covers. We bought ten each of the creeping phlox *Phlox stolonifera* 'Bruce's White', 'Home Fires', 'Blue Ridge', and 'Sherwood Purple' and interplanted them

4.9 MAY *The beech tunnel acts as a coupler between the Woodland Garden and the bottom of the Long Borders, so we repeated many of the same plants on both sides of the tunnel.*

among species *Tiarella cordifolia* as well as the hybrid *T.* 'Slick Rock', the blue *Phlox divaricata* and the white hybrid *P. d.* 'Dirgo Ice', and *Ajuga reptans* 'Caitlin's Giant', so we had a carpet of blue, pink, and white, then for a few years interplanted them with tulips (4.4).

In another, moister section of the woodland by the Colombian urn, we planted divisions of cinnamon fern (*Osmunda cinnamomea*) that the late Carol Laise Bunker, a client, gave me years ago. One day Carol asked me to divide the cinnamon ferns that her late husband, Ellsworth Bunker, had had planted thirty years before, and offered me some of the divisions. I accepted, knowing that Alice Holway, another of my mentors, had planted them for Carol's late husband. Alice had been Senator George Aiken's plantswoman at the Putney Nursery for more than thirty years. These humble native ferns were drawing together associations in my mind; I was a young adult during the Vietnam War when Mr. Bunker was the U.S. ambassador to Vietnam and Senator Aiken was an outspoken critic of that war.

To complement those far-ranging associations, I planted several clumps of another plant that Alice Holway had given me—the double form of white trillium (*Trillium grandiflorum*)—next to the ferns. Because Howard Andros had introduced me to Alice Holway, I planted nearby a ring of seven tiny February daphne (*Daphne mezereum*) seedlings that Howard gave us. Today, those seven form what looks like a single 6-foot-diameter shrub 4 feet high. When they are in bloom, we catch their fragrance a hundred feet away, and that fragrance is now all caught up with our memories of Alice and Howard.

The Double Bloodroot

WE ALSO PLANTED several sweeps of thirty to fifty double bloodroot (*Sanguinaria canadensis* 'Flore Pleno'), and herein lies another deep association I feel. The hundreds of double bloodroot that now thrive in our woodland all came from ten or so rhizomes that Howard Andros had given me when I was first starting as a professional garden designer in the early 1980s.

Back in the 1940s, when Howard was just getting started with

Spring in the Woodland

1. SPRING *The shocking pink of* Rhododendron *'Aglo' provides a powerful contrast with the woodland phlox.*

2. SPRING *Without 'Aglo', the woodland feels quieter, gentler. Take your pick.*

his landscape design and installation business, a friend of his had found a double bloodroot that had sixty-four, not the normal eight, petals. It was not so much a double form of bloodroot as a square of it. Howard planted that precious single rhizome, then in September of the following year dug it up and divided it. Then he had two. The next year he divided the rhizomes and he had four. He continued this careful husbandry of those rhizomes for well over forty years and became one of the country's primary suppliers of *Sanguinaria canadensis* 'Flore Pleno' for major mail-order catalogs. We carry on Howard's thrifty approach to plants by digging up all our rhizomes every other year and dividing and replanting them in replenished soil. I will never forget looking at a drift of these fleeting 1-inch-diameter globes of sixty-four pure white petals held atop delicate 3-inch stems one April in our Woodland Garden. I said to Howard, "It's such a shame these blooms last for only a few days," and Howard replied, "Anything that beautiful can't last."

Other Plants

OVER THE PAST TWENTY YEARS, we have continued to add plants to broaden the appeal of our Woodland Garden. We planted bulbs of *Fritillaria meleagris* to complement the blooms of daffodils we had planted the year before (4.5). We planted *Hosta* 'Sum and Substance' to create a visual link between it and the chartreuse-leaved *Hosta* 'Sun Power' in the Brick Walk Garden. We interspersed *Euphorbia polychroma*, with its acid green flowers, to create a striking contrast with the woodland phlox bloom. Then, to provide midsummer bloom, we planted white and pink astilbes next to lavender-flowering hostas (4.6), sweet pepperbush (*Clethra alnifolia*), with its fragrant white blooms in late summer, and Harry Lauder's walking stick (*Corylus avellana* 'Contorta') in a sunny spot near the gazebo. Sweet cicely (*Myrrhis odorata*) went in near the entrance to one of the paths so we would brush against it and release the anise fragrance. And so it goes, plants upon plants, all held together by a strong, subtle structure, with stone wall and meadow as background.

5

The Long Borders
and the Three Oaks

HAVING THINNED OUT TREES, saplings, and brush along the south stone wall in preparation for starting the Woodland Garden, we took a new look at the expanse of lawn stretching north from the southeast corner of the overall garden (J on map). What would we do with this area? Again, we looked at existing features surrounding this area to help us design it. To the west was the line of the Brick Walk Garden; to the east was an old stone wall that, like the one to the south, separated our growing garden from the east and south meadows. But the key to this area turned out to be to the south, where a well-shaped maple tree and a black locust about 30 feet apart framed a view over the stone wall and across the meadow. The meadow sloped away to a view of tree lines and hill ridges folding into the distance toward the town of Brattleboro, some 15 miles south.

Frame Views

VIEWS BECOME PART OF THE GARDEN only when they are framed. The frame we made with the two mature trees turned out to have many implications for our burgeoning garden. First, we put a large sitting stone in the cleared area between the locust and maple, then planted an orchard: pairs of apple trees, pear trees, peach trees, and plum trees. The fruit was delicious, but it had been a bad design decision, one that we grew beyond in a year. We transplanted the fruit trees to the field across the road,

5.1 MAY *The gazebo introduces the all-important elements of shelter and destination, while also framing views into the garden.*

Seasons in the Long Borders: 1. SPRING 1985 *Just after we removed the lawn to form beds and path.*
2. SPRING 2003 *Including the sitting area in the west border.* 3. AUTUMN *Autumn in the borders.*

4. WINTER *Evergreens, grasses, and the gazebo are the focus.*

but a design seed had been sown: pairs of gardens running north-south that would line up with the gap between the two trees.

Look to Gardens You've Visited

MARY, NATE, AND I had visited no end of gardens in England, but it was the one closest to Mary's heart—the Hidcote Manor Gardens—that we turned to for inspiration as to how to create this hybrid Old England–New England garden. First, we thought of how Lawrence Johnston, an American, had set out a pair of red borders at Hidcote on either side of a central lawn. The lawn leads to a set of steps between a pair of gazebos.

We also thought about the grand beech allée that started from one of those two gazebos and stretched away on a broad central lawn between great beech hedges. That central lawn ended in a pair of magnificent wrought-iron gates. Even today we can stand between those gates and look across the field of wheat, barley, or oats to the hamlet of Hidcote Boyce and Mary's brother Simon's barns and the house where Mary grew up. Lawrence Johnston's magnificent gardens in Gloucestershire and other such grand gardens can provide inspiration for our far more modest efforts.

We cut beds out of lawn (page 110: 1) in such a way as to leave an 8-foot-wide path between them. Once the panels of lawn were removed, we rototilled in compost in preparation for planting. Given that these borders ran north-south and are in one of the sunnier parts of the garden, we knew that whatever we planted in them would get even sunlight throughout the day. Now that the orchard was gone, I suggested we plant pairs of trees up the length of those beds and underplant with simple ground covers to create a spare English allée. Mary and Nate thought that was boring and held out for a more complex garden of shrubs and perennials. We did plant five pairs of Kousa dogwoods (*Cornus kousa*) 15 feet apart down the length of the two borders as a structure plant, but at one point during their second winter the temperature dropped to –25 degrees Fahrenheit with howling winds on more than one night, and that was the end of the Kousas.

111

New Shapes from Old Ones

IN CREATING THIS STRONG, 8-foot-wide central panel of lawn with borders on either side, we resolved some of the irregularities to the east and west of the borders. Although the 40-foot-diameter circular lawn around the apple tree insinuated itself into the back of the west border, it wasn't too much of a problem because the bed was deep enough to accommodate the bulge of lawn in its west side (See map where areas J and F meet).

Knowing we wanted to sit in the Long Borders, Nate, then twelve, suggested that we create a set of stone steps that would lead up to a stone-paved sitting area with a hedge around its back to separate the Brick Walk Garden from the top of the Long Borders (5.3 and 5.7).

We set two broad stone steps that lead from the lawn path up to a bluestone-paved sitting area. To increase the feeling of separation from other parts of the garden, we planted a broadly arcing hedge of the evergreen *Chamaecyparis pisifera* 'Filifera' around the back, then set three small English hedge maples (*Acer campestre*) in a gap in the hedge just behind the central bench for contrast: the frilly, ferny *Chamaecyparis* next to the shorn hedge maples. We then planted a birch tree (*Betula platyphylla japonica*) by the steps for shade. By repeating that distinctive tree deep into the garden, we set up a visual relationship between it and the two whitespire birches at either end of the Entry Garden, a relationship that can be seen from many parts of the garden because of the distinctive shape and bark color of the white birch.

Drama and Architecture

ONCE THE TWO BORDERS WERE PREPARED, we felt that the simple bench between the two trees was no longer up to the task of being the culminating object at the end of two dramatic 90-foot-long borders. It was clear that we needed a structure that would be in keeping with the borders and the panel of lawn, and thereby act with the garden shed as bookends to this section of the garden.

We contacted Roger Kahle, a friend and superb carpenter-craftsman-designer, and together we designed and Roger built this most important new structure in the garden. It made all the differ-

5.2 *(above)* SPRING 1984
Gordon establishes the edges of the Long Borders with his grandmother's straight-nosed spade.

ence. Crafted from oak and hemlock beams and shingled with cedar shakes, the gazebo felt right in the woodland at the bottom of the garden. By lining up this 10-foot by 10-foot structure on the center of the 8-foot-wide lawn path, it fit into the plan for the existing garden. But its placement between maple and locust would not have become apparent to us had we not cleared the saplings from between those two major trees in the first place. It's all a question of seeing, of paying attention.

5.3 *(below)* JUNE *Nate, our son, suggested we create a sitting area right in the border so we could sit among our plants, not just walk by them.*

Four Seasons in the Gazebo, Looking North: 1. SPRING *A terra-cotta urn acting as a focal point.* 2. SUMMER *When color and texture overflow.* 3. AUTUMN *When foliage colors in trees overhead glow.* 4. WINTER *A study in green and white, beige and gray.*

Destinations

WE PURPOSELY HAD NOT PROVIDED a place to sit in the Brick Walk Garden, under the apple tree, or in the Woodland Garden. There was no place we wanted a chair or bench except perhaps in the back of the Woodland Garden. We didn't want to overdo chairs and benches. We also didn't want to see more than one sitting area from most spots in the garden. The gazebo is the first destination with furniture along our itinerary, in part because the views from it are so strong. Furthermore, the gazebo was the focus of the Beech Tunnel as well as the focus of the central path down the Long Borders, so we could see those chairs from other significant parts of the garden (pages 114–15).

This turned out to be the most dramatic of our five sitting areas, partly because the four corner posts frame expansive views in four directions. As we enter the gazebo from the Beech Tunnel, we look south across the meadow to a view 10 to 15 miles south to the Connecticut River Valley. Sitting on the north-facing bench, we look up the length of the two 90-foot-long borders. Sitting on the east-facing chair, we look under the maple tree and out across the meadow to the bench under the Three Oaks. Sit on the west-facing chair and we look into the Beech Tunnel and across the Woodland Garden (5.1). Each view has its own special time of year, but the view north is particularly good in mid-October when the foliage changes.

Create Shelter

THE GAZEBO is the only sitting area in the garden with a solid roof. We sit under its shelter in a light summer rain listening to the splash on the cedar shakes, or relax in its shade on a hot summer evening and feel a gentle, cool breeze at our backs as it flows up the meadow and through the open sides of the gazebo. But perhaps the most magic moment of all is when we can sit in the gazebo after sunset and watch the moon come up over the east ridgeline of the meadow.

Borrow Views

ONE EVENING just after we installed the gazebo, we were sitting in it looking north through a frame created by the gazebo uprights and its roof and floor. We realized we could see through or over trees, shrubs, and hedges to the top of the south-facing gable end of our house to the left of the frame. In the center of the frame we could see the much smaller gable end of our garden shed some 200 feet away. Then we looked more closely to the right and realized that with simple pruning we could expose a view of the gable end of our neighbor Howard Prussack's barn, at least a quarter of a mile away across the Ranney cornfield (9.11). I cut a few branches from a maple tree in the middle ground and a few saplings across the road more than 400 feet from the gazebo, pruned a few branches to open more of a view of the house and

5.4 OCTOBER *The plumes of* Miscanthus sinensis *'Purpurascens' and the deep pink blooms of* Eupatorium maculatum *'Gateway' celebrate autumn in the Long Borders.*

shed, then went to sit in the gazebo again. With 20 minutes of simple pruning, we created a view of three gable ends of three old buildings, thereby defining depth within as well as at a considerable distance from our garden. Those gable ends became the visual anchor when looking at the garden from the gazebo, a place we often visit. It was simply a question of seeing.

We were so pleased with what we had just discovered that we thought we'd try another vantage point. Mary sat in the west-facing chair and looked through its frame to the west. With a bit of pruning high in two maples on our property some 150 feet across McKinnon Road, we could frame a view of the ridgeline of what they call here in Vermont a "high mowing"—that is, a hilltop meadow nearly a mile away. This was clearly a good idea. With an extension ladder and saw, I set myself up some 30 feet off the ground and between the two trees. Mary gave me directions from the chair as to which limbs to cut, and within minutes I had removed about ten branches to clear a 15-foot-wide, 35-foot-high notch in the trees that enabled us to see across the valley to the Ranney's high mowing.

Limit Furniture Materials

A FEELING OF UNITY comes in part from the fact that we have limited ourselves to teak furniture, although the chairs and benches vary in design from area to area. (Our chairs, benches, and tables have "Smartwood Certification," so we know they are made of plantation-grown wood.) We use teak because we can leave it out in all weather during the gardening season and because it ages a silvery gray, the same color as our house. Over time, gray lichens grow on it, adding to an established, settled feeling. Furthermore, by repeating this one wood in all furniture, we set up a repetition of material that underpins coherence across the garden.

There is one exception. Last year, Mary painted all four of my grandmother's folding metal chairs royal blue. We put two in the sitting area at the top of one of the borders and the other two in the Herb Garden. These blue chairs look striking against the greens and grays of the garden, and add an unexpected punch of color. When this section of our garden appeared on the cover of *Fine*

Gardening magazine in February 2003, an equal number of readers told me how much they liked the blue chairs as told me how much they didn't like them. Well, Mary and I are pleased—in fact, as the English would say, "chuffed"—by what we regard as the success of our blue chairs.

Choose Plants for Pleasing Contrast

WHEN IT CAME TIME to choose plants for the Long Borders, we followed the same sequence we followed for the Brick Walk Garden, though we certainly paid a lot more attention to the look of these borders across the entire growing season, given their important position in the garden.

We started by choosing a strong structural plant, remembering how successfully Lawrence Johnston at Hidcote had planted pairs of arborvitae (*Thuja occidentalis*) 20 feet or so apart as structural plants down the length of both rose gardens. As I mentioned, we tried *Cornus kousa* as the main structural plant, but their second winter "put paid," as the English say, to that idea. We then decided to repeat pairs of purple-leaved barberries (*Berberis thunbergii* 'Atropurpurea') down the length of each border.

The passage of time has created a problem for us. *Berberis thunbergii* in its many forms is now on the national list of invasive plants, which one should avoid planting. We like its strong red leaves, not only because they match the color of the south-facing front door of the house but because they stand out well against green-leaved plants, thereby creating pleasing contrast. This past year we took out the barberries and replaced them with the purple-leaved ninebark (*Physocarpus opulifolius* Diabolo™).

Having chosen this primary structural plant, we turned to large-scale herbaceous plants to support the ninebarks in their role as structural elements. We set the ornamental grasses *Miscanthus sinensis* 'Purpurascens,' *M. s.* 'Variegatus', and *M. s.* 'Morning Light' here and there down the length of the borders for their strong form and marvelous fall effect (5.5). We designed two places for hybrids of the 7-foot-high Joe Pye weed (*Eupatorium maculatum* 'Gateway') (5.6)—at the top of one bed and the bottom of the other—then set out three to five of the large-leaved *Crambe*

5.5 EARLY OCTOBER
Our garden's last hurrah.

cordifolia and purple-leaved snakeroot (*Actaea simplex* 'Atropurpurea') in various places down the length of both beds.

Once we had chosen places for these major herbaceous plants, we dropped down to midsize herbaceous plants that would offer flower as well as foliage from May through the summer until all the fall-blooming structural plants came into their own.

Having chosen the structural plants for May, June, July, and August, we selected smaller perennials that would bloom with their larger structural neighbors. You will see many of these combinations in Appendix C, on plants in our Vermont garden. We also took advantage of a design principle I've written of earlier: theme and variation.

Because the front door of our house is dark red, we chose the theme of burgundy or dark red foliage to vary judiciously throughout the garden to link garden to house. The variation came from the many red-leaved shrubs and perennials we planted in the Long Borders: *Physocarpus opulifolius* 'Diablo' *Penstemon digitalis* 'Husker's Red'; *Actaea simplex* 'Atropurpurea'; dark red Asiatic lilies; various dark red coleus in pots followed in September by dark red chrysanthemums such as 'Helen'; *Heuchera* 'Chocolate Ruffles', 'Cascade Dawn', and 'Stormy Seas' or *Heuchera micrantha* 'Palace Purple'; and, of course, the purple-leaved Beech Tunnel.

Formal Shapes Set Off Informal Ones

BEING SHORN, the Beech Tunnel stands in direct contrast to the natural forms of the nearby stewartia and all the hostas and ground covers surrounding the tunnel. The shorn English hedge maples at the north end of the Long Borders do the same thing, yet more powerfully. By shearing these three 16-foot-high trees, two into teardrops and the middle one to a lower flat panel, we create formality and a level of contrast that functions across the whole southern half of the garden. These geometric shapes stand in pleasing contrast not only to the frilly *Chamaecyparis* hedge into which they are set but to the free forms of the nearby apple tree, the dwarf white pine, the red-twigged dogwoods, the ornamental grasses, and the white birch only 10 feet away. When sitting in the gazebo we look north, and there in the midst of all the visual activ-

5.6 (opposite) EARLY OCTOBER *Just before I have to rake 259,765,392 leaves from the garden.*

5.7 (overleaf) MAY *The sitting area at the top of the Long Borders, with* Rhododendron *'Molly Fordham' at her peak.*

ity of two 90-foot-long borders stand two anchoring elements: the teardrop hedge maples and the long, horizontal *Viburnum prunifolium* hedge along the south side of the Herb Garden. These shorn plants act as centers, as visual anchors that contrast with the natural forms around them.

Color Links and Focal Points

TO UNDERPIN the link between the gazebo and the next area along the itinerary—the shady Rock Garden—we set a light-colored, two-handled terra-cotta urn by the steps into the rock garden. The urn emphasizes the strong visual relationship between gazebo, borders, and rock garden that we had already established with the lawn path (page 114: 1). Furthermore, by the simple act of pruning to expose the gable end of our neighbor's barn to a view from the gazebo, we underscored the relationship of all parts of the garden on that long sight line between the gazebo and the barn a quarter mile to the north.

Repeat Materials and Plants for Coherence

WE ALSO REPEATED materials in the Long Borders that we used elsewhere in the garden: teak furniture; mica schist for the steps into the gazebo as well as onto the sitting area within the north end of the borders; bluestone and brick as the paving materials to support the bench, table, and chairs in that same sitting area; pea stone as the base for pots under an ash tree; and lawn paths that run north between the Long Borders and on to all other parts of the garden. Finally, there was the stone wall, the lasting edge that formed the backdrop for both the Long Borders and the south edge of the Woodland Garden. We repeated stone walls in new gardens behind the house, but more on that later.

We also repeated certain key plants in the Long Borders that had appeared earlier along our itinerary: *Miscanthus* grasses in variety; boxwood (*Buxus* 'Green Mountain') that we used to mark the four corners at the top of the Long Borders (5.7); whitespire birch, which we planted at either end of the yew hedge in the Entry Garden as well as in the north sitting area in the Long Borders; and Joe Pye weed, which would reappear in the Pool Garden. The list could go on. It is a list that confirms those stronger elements of coherence: paths, view lines, built structures, stone walls, and backgrounds.

Vertical Trees in a Horizontal Landscape

WHILE DEVELOPING our garden over twenty years, we were aware of the beauty of the meadows and the role they played as a gentle background. Early on we decided to plant three pin oaks (*Quercus palustris*) in the south meadow, then mow and maintain a path from a gap in the stone wall (L on map, and page 127) out to and around those pin oaks some 300 feet or so into the meadow. In creating that path and circle, and setting a bench under those oaks, we co-opted our meadow into a strong visual and physical relationship with the garden and reinforced our sentiment that the meadow is part of the garden. The bench and path were there to invite us to venture into that feature in the broad landscape. As wonderful as it is to sit in our designed garden, it is

5.8 JUNE *The Long Borders in high summer, when it's all a riot of weaving and flopping and falling and spikes and mounds.*

equally wonderful to sit in the hayfield—mown and baled two or three times a year by Harold or his son Philip—and watch the moon rise or the sun set or just look down the wooded valley toward Brattleboro. Sitting on the bench among the three oaks in the meadow makes us feel, perhaps more than any other part of our garden, that we are part of the place where we live. This pastoral setting is made all the more beautiful by the sight and sound of swallows swooping over the meadow, the sight of dragonfly wings catching the evening sunlight, and the fragrance of the meadow grasses after a hot summer day as we sit in the cooling shade of the oaks.

Benches Define Depth

THE BENCH under the pin oaks (page 127) also had a profound impact on perceiving distance. The day we set the bench, we sat on it for a bit, then walked to the garden to look back to the three oaks. The bench had changed everything. As I stood in the garden looking across the 300-foot distance to the bench, for the first time I understood and felt how far away those oak trees were. Nothing else in the landscape around that circle of oaks helped us gauge distance. Why? Because we know roughly how big a bench is, but how big is an oak? How wide is a lawn path? You can't tell, so you can't understand distance. When I grasped just what was at work with that bench in the meadow, I understood how important it is to use objects of known size to help define depth and distance in a garden.

5.9 AUGUST *Love Lies a Bleeding, a drama queen in a blue pot.*

**The Three Oaks in
Three Seasons**

1. MAY *1,284,716 dandelions
in bloom in the meadow.*

2. LATE MAY
*1,284,716 dandelions
in full seed not 100 feet
from our garden.*

3. AUTUMN *October
light in Vermont is change-
able and full of drama.*

6

The Rock Garden
and the Dining Area

WE MOVED INTO OUR HOUSE on December 1, 1983. Just as we pulled in that late afternoon, the operator of the huge well-drilling rig, having completed his job to a depth of 225 feet, was churning his truck through mud from the well site on the west edge of what would become our rock garden. He had to maneuver his mammoth vehicle across a hundred feet of muddy lawn and eventually did so, leaving 18-inch-deep ruts that immediately froze and filled with snow. The next morning the plumbers arrived to fit the lines and submersible pump while, with his backhoe, Bill Fitzpatrick dug a 5-foot-deep trench from the well to the foundation of the house. The plumbers laid their lines, Bill backfilled the trench, and when they all left we had a muddy mess frozen in place, *but* we had running water.

With the thaw in the spring of 1984, we started the cleanup of the well-drilling operation at the edge of what we discovered was a roughly 3-foot-high mound of rocks 30 feet long and 15 feet wide that sloped down at the north and south ends. Years later we learned that this had been a ramp onto which horses pulled skids affixed to a wooden vat filled with maple sap. Each late winter, when the sap was running, the Ranneys would gravity-feed this sap into the evaporating pan set within a little shack where they would boil it down to maple syrup. (We would unearth that 12-foot-long crumpled metal pan when removing brambles from the area that summer.)

6.1 MAY *Part of the magic of this dining area comes from sitting in a shady, enclosed place looking out at the sunny, expansive meadow.*

THE ROCK GARDEN

Old Features in a New Garden

RATHER THAN have a backhoe remove this mound of rock, we asked Ellis Derrig to add more boulders to its edge to create shallow terraces. He left three gaps among the boulders on the south, west, and north sides for rustic steps that I would build shortly thereafter on a line with the existing paths. We then backfilled with topsoil so we could turn this mound into a garden.

We now walk up the central lawn path of the Long Borders where we first see the two-handled urn, then ascend the south steps that lead onto the top of the Rock Garden. When walking from the Entry Garden and through the Orchard, we look east between the first two rows of crab apples to the west steps leading from the lawn onto the mound. When leaving the Herb Garden through the south break in the *Viburnum prunifolium* hedge, we need to walk across only a few feet of lawn to the north set of steps (page 131: 2) that lead onto the mound, from where we enjoy a view down the length of the Long Borders to the gazebo (6.2).

Because I used stones that wick up water to build these three sets of steps, within a year they were covered with moss and receded into green ground cover. To draw attention to the steps, I used vertical elements. I marked the steps at the south end with a terra-cotta urn. For the west steps, I set a standing stone that Harold Ranney had given us just to the right of the bottom step, then planted a small Korean fir next to it. The fir provided some context for this vertical element and created an interplay of material and plant (6.3). At either side of the north bottom step, I set short vertical stones, then planted the almost white foliaged *Pulmonaria* 'Majesty' next to one of them (6.4).

Higher Vantage Points

THE STEPS visually and physically link three existing areas of the garden to this rocky garden and also draw us onto the mound. Because the Rock Garden is 4 feet above adjacent lawn, being up there provides us with a different viewpoint. Just this little difference in height gives us the opportunity to look down on

Three Seasons in the Rock Garden

1. SPRING *Looking south from the quiet rock garden to the dramatic borders.*

2. AUTUMN *Maples blaze, showering the whole garden in reds, yellows, and oranges.*

3. WINTER *White snow on green shrubs and gray limbs.*

6.2 MAY *The path up and onto the Rock Garden draws guests to this highest vantage point in the garden.*

6.3 *(above right)* SUMMER
Abies koreana *cones and foliage
pleasingly contrast with a
calcareous schist fencepost
Harold Ranney gave us.*

parts of the garden, especially the Dining Area to the east and the Long Borders to the south.

The east side of the Rock Garden was the most difficult side of the mound to manage. It sloped so steeply and was so rough that we had to rebuild one retaining wall and add a second (6.5). We called Joe Fichter, a sculptor and art teacher at the nearby Putney School who was looking for wall-building work that summer. He rebuilt the upper wall, then built a second retaining wall below it from stone we had been stockpiling as we cleaned up the place. This lower wall served as a sideboard for the dining area we eventually created next to it. The result of all this work was that we now had a level surface on the top of the mound and a second level

planting shelf on the east side of the Rock Garden. Level surfaces are always better than sloping ones for planting and maintenance.

Structure in this area, then, came from the three steps, the paths from them that converged on the top of the mound, the two retaining walls, and the boulder walls along the other three sides. The resulting form was already so strong that we did not need to establish structure with plants the way we'd had to in the Long Borders and the Brick Walk Garden.

We couldn't do much to change the quickly draining soil atop these boulders, but we could effect semishade. We removed all the lower branches of the maples in that area up to a height of 12 feet or so, thereby allowing morning and afternoon light to reach the plants beneath them sooner and for longer periods of time.

To deal with the quick drainage, we added topsoil in the gaps

6.4 *(previous spread)* JULY *Granite upright stones leading up to the Rock Garden give rise to lichens; pumicey calcareous schist steps wick up water to support moss and ferns.*

6.5 *(below)* MAY *While our garden is a series of distinct areas, none except the Herb Garden is hedged from sight. We like generous views into other areas of the garden, as here, from the Dining Area through the Long Borders to the gazebo.*

between the boulders, and chose plants appropriate for such conditions. We were not about to irrigate this or any other part of the garden. The plants would have to make it on their own.

Right Plant for the Situation

THE BOULDERS established a relaxed, organic feeling to the garden, so we chose plants accordingly. We started with a dwarf Scots pine (*Pinus sylvestris* 'Nana'), knowing that it would grow far more slowly for lack of deep topsoil than the one in the Brick Walk Garden and therefore stay in scale with this relatively small garden area. We underplanted it with a spreading yew (*Taxus baccata* 'Repandens') on one side and several gray-leaved Japanese garden juniper (*Juniperus procumbens* 'Nana'), both of which can thrive in half a day of sun. We also planted three small

6.6 OCTOBER

Serendipitous moments occur when a twig from a nearby Acer pseudosieboldiana *intertwines with that of a Korean fir.*

137

Korean fir (*Abies koreana*), knowing that they too would grow slowly in this challenging situation. We planted five shade- and sun-tolerant Russian cypress (*Microbiota decussata*) along the top of the upper stone wall so their ferny foliage would cover and drape over the top of the wall.

With these and other evergreens planted, we turned to deciduous shrubs and small trees. We put in a Korean maple (*Acer pseudo-sieboldianum*) to contrast with a Korean fir, a combination that is especially beautiful in autumn when the maple leaves turn brilliant red (6.6). Several Shibori spirea (*Spiraea japonica* 'Shibori') went in next to the Russian cypress, again for foliage contrast. Then we massed heaths (Erica) at the protected base of north-facing boulders.

A small star magnolia (*Magnolia stellata*) went in near the north steps in semishade. By planting it there, not more than 6 feet from the trunk of the large maple, we knew it would grow slowly because it had to compete with the maple. To ensure that it stays small, I prune any upright branches and encourage all horizontal branches, so we have a lovely 5-foot-high dwarflike magnolia.

Once trees and shrubs were in, we chose drought- and shade-tolerant perennials and ground covers. We put in a few starter plants of the dark burgundy-leaved *Viola labradorica* in the gaps between the south-facing steps (6.7); they've now naturalized throughout the area. We planted *Lamium maculatum* 'White Nancy' along the edges of the south steps as well as dwarf rockcress (*Arabis sturii*), and also encouraged moss to grow throughout this naturalistic garden.

6.7 LATE SUMMER
These granite steps leading to the Rock Garden are so completely integrated into the scene that we marked the entrance with this vertical cast stone pedestal.

Seasons in the Dining Area: 1. EARLY SUMMER *Before the mosquitoes hatch, we have lunch out here.* 2. LATE SUMMER *After a month or so, the mosquitoes are mostly gone and we eat out here for the rest of the summer.* 3. AUTUMN *Chilly evenings mean we*

use this area for lunch on weekends.
4. WINTER *On a quiet, sunny day.*

THE DINING AREA

Edges for the Looking

THE EDGES of this area adjacent to the Rock Garden were already established: a stone retaining wall that Joe Fichter built to the west; a curving stone wall and black cherry and maple trees to the east and north; and a huge ash tree at the top of the Long Borders to the south. Given that mature trees ringed this roughly 30-foot-diameter area, one of the first things we did was to high-prune all the trees so their lowest branches would be around 20 feet off the ground (pages 140–41). In this way, we opened views to the nearby gardens and meadows and brought in more light.

As we were preparing the soil for planting, we unearthed hundreds of whole and broken bricks that had once been the sugarhouse where the early Ranneys had boiled down maple sap. We used the sound bricks—two with mink paw prints in them—to rebuild one of the chimneys in the house; we hauled away the broken bits.

Then we tried to garden in this ring of maples. This is one case when exerting our will turned into a fool's errand. All the clues were there not to garden this area: matted maple roots that came up with every shovelful of broken brick; gravelly soil; full shade; no moisture. Did we pay attention? No. Did we lay down stone and use the area as a shaded dining spot? Well, we did, but only after five or so years of beating our heads against rock maples.

Site Sitting Areas

ONE SUMMER, after years of trying to garden in this ring of maples, my installation crew and I had traveled to East Hampton, on the tip of Long Island, to install a Japanese-style dry streambed garden for our friend and client Dory Small. As we were laying the trailer load of mica schist, Dory showed me a pile of cut bluestone she no longer wanted. Would I like to take the stone back to Vermont? Her offer changed the outcome of our dining area. When I got home, Mary and I uprooted those few perennials struggling under the maples and in the gravel, spread 2 inches of sand, and laid Dory's bluestone.

We bought a teak dining table and chairs. One night shortly after we had set up the dining area, we asked friends Peter and Theodora Berg and Nick and Joan Thorndike for dinner; we knew we had finally found the right use for this space when, as we were serving dessert that June night, the full moon rose over the east ridgeline. It was one of those stunning moments in a garden, the kind we'll never forget.

At the edge of this new Dining Area was a butternut that was clearly struggling. We had to sweep fallen twigs and leaves from the table, chairs, and bluestone daily. One day that summer, Nate and I got out our chain saw and ladders and started taking down the tree. Mary came out as we were working and suggested that we leave 8 feet or so of the trunk intact, perhaps to support a vine.

A few days later Mary showed me a book about The Green Man, a Druidic symbol of the place where the world of people and plants intersect. She suggested we hire friend and sculptor Gerry Prozzo to carve the face of a Green Man into what remained of the trunk (6.9). What better symbol for a garden could there be? We arranged a barter: Gerry would do the carving and we would help him and his wife, Cyndy, maintain their garden for the year. When the trunk, still solid in the ground after ten years, eventually rots out, we'll mount the sound part of the trunk on stone.

Sculpture Draws the Eye

A COUPLE YEARS after Gerry carved the Green Man, we were visiting designer Anthony Paul's garden south of London. Anthony has created 10 acres of gardens around connected ponds; his wife, Hannah Peschar, a sculpture gallery owner, displays the work of sculptors from across England and Europe in the garden.

Because the Green Man proved a strong male figure in our garden, we had been looking for an equally strong female figure, and that day among Hannah's collection in Anthony's garden we saw it: a black ceramic bust titled *Hero*, by English sculptor Patricia Volk. According to Greek myth, Hero waited in vain for her lover, Lysander, to swim the Hellespont to be with her. We shipped *Hero* across the Atlantic and set her on the stone wall just above eye

6.8 *(opposite)* SUMMER *Patricia Volk, a sculptor from Wiltshire, England, made this introspective ceramic bust of Hero that presides over the Dining Area.*

6.9 *(below)* SUMMER *Our friend Gerry Prozzo carved the Green Man, a Druidic image to symbolize the meeting place between the world of human beings and plants, into the trunk of a dead butternut tree in our dining area.*

level overlooking the Dining Area (6.8) facing the Green Man. The day she was placed, she became a major visual reference point and a powerful spirit in the garden.

Quiet Plants for Quiet Places

WITH THE WALLS, paving, and sculpture in place, we began planting the perimeter so we could sit at our dining table within a garden. We started with the little terrace behind the west retaining wall. Given the shade and quickly draining soil, we planted a collection of hostas interspersed with the silver-variegated *Lamium galeobdolon* 'Herman's Pride'. We chose a climbing hydrangea (*Hydrangea petiolaris*) for the trunk of a black cherry tree as well as along the top of a stone wall. We planted a pair of boxwood (*Buxus microphylla* 'Green Mountain') on either side of the entrance to the Dining Area, and backed them up with cast concrete baskets of fruit.

We brought light and color into this shady, enclosed spot with two 26-inch-diameter terra-cotta pots planted differently each year, sometimes with the yellow-variegated *Hosta* 'Shade Fanfare' along with the yellow-blooming *Kirengeshoma palmata*, at other times with *coleus* (*Solenostemon* 'Alabama Sunset', 6.11) and other combinations of annuals.

The Sound of Water

TO EMPHASIZE the peace of this area, we wanted to introduce the sound of water, but we weren't sure how. At Whichford Pottery that summer, we saw a lovely water feature that included a bowl for water atop a pedestal. Water, stored in a buried basin hidden by small rounded stones, was pumped up through the hollow core of the pedestal and filled the urn, then spilled over its edges, down onto the rounded river rocks and back into the hidden basin. When we got back to Vermont, we made a smaller version. Now we sit with friends in the Dining Area, our conversation mixed with the sound of flowing water (6.10).

When purchasing the cast concrete urn for the bubbler, we bought a second matching one and blocked its central hole with hydraulic cement. When we have guests, we fill it with water and

6.10 *(above)* SUMMER
This bubbler provides just a hint of the sound of falling water near our dining table.

6.11 *(opposite)* AUGUST
Coleus *'Alabama Sunset' strikes a vibrant note while in the background the sculpture and the shorn tops of the English hedge maples provide a firm contrast to the many textures around them.*

float flowers to bring color, a hint of the larger garden, and the reflection of the trees into the otherwise quiet Dining Area (6.12).

Link Gardens

IT WAS EASY to establish the relationship between Dining Area and adjacent gardens. The top portion of the Long Borders simply flowed in under the branches of the high-pruned maples, visually and physically linking these two garden areas; the bubbler served as the linchpin. The relationship between Dining Area and Rock Garden was confirmed by the two stone retaining walls and *Hero* sitting atop the uppermost of the two looking down into the Dining Area. The entry between the two boxwoods leads left into the Herb Garden or right toward the Spring Garden; path leads to path, pulling the parts into physical and visual relationships with one another.

6.12 AUGUST *When guests come for lunch or dinner, we mark the occasion by floating flowers from the garden in this urn in the Dining Area.*

7

The Herb Garden

BESIDES THE HOUSE with its attached barn, the only other building on the place when we arrived in 1983 was a 12-foot by 18-foot weathered shed that had been built more than a hundred years ago to dry tobacco (7.2). It was filled with boards, wire, old windows, glass panes, broken tools, cans of oil and creosote, bits of rope, and jars of screws, bolts, and nails. The roof was covered with rotten wooden shingles, but somehow the structure and charm of this lovely little building remained intact.

Adjacent to it were the remnants of a one-and-a-half-story barn, perhaps 20 feet square, that was beyond repair. The rusty metal roof provided some degree of shelter for 5- to 6-foot-high piles of old boards of every length, width, and condition you can imagine, as well as rolls of electrical and barbed wire and buckets and cans. While sorting through this tangle that first winter, we found a heavy-duty building jack under the sound remnants of one corner post. Once we had removed all the boards from the barn, I tied a chain to the jack, which was frozen with rust, and pulled on it with my pickup truck. The barn lurched, leaned, and held itself in midair. With a chain saw, I cut through the remaining corner posts and the thing fell in a heap. I put some of the metal roofing panels on the shed and took the balance to the recycling center.

Small Garden, Small Building

THE PROPORTION AND DIMENSIONS, the shape and materials of the shed itself helped us design the Herb Garden, the enclosing hedges, and the peony and geranium bed to the east, and the placement of garden ornaments within. In a larger sense, the design for the gardens around this small building had a ripple effect, influencing designs for subsequent areas adjacent to it.

We had been thinking about where to site a traditional grape arbor and herb garden; the back, or east side, of this shed seemed the perfect place for both, in part because the scale of the building was right for the intimate garden we envisioned. The shed would shelter a sitting area under the arbor from the predominant west wind. During the hot months of July and August, the arbor could shade the bench from late morning through noon; then the shed itself would provide afternoon and evening shade.

Without worrying about what the next step would be, we asked our friends Victor Olson and Sparrow Hart to build us a rustic arbor based on the shed's materials and dimensions. They centered the arbor on the shed's 16-foot-long wall, built its upper deck at the

7.1 (previous spread) JUNE *Our classic four-quadrant herb garden fit neatly into a space on the east side of our old garden shed.*

7.2 (above) MARCH 1984 *We made progress over the winter of 1983–84, but the place was still bleak. (See 2.2 to see what the south side of the house looked like in October 1983.)*

7.3 JULY 1995 *A weathered old shed gave rise to an informal garden and an unpainted grape arbor supported by locust posts. The shed sets the mood.*

same height as that of the shed's east wall, and made the uprights from black locust posts to echo the other uses to which we had put this material throughout the garden. When they had completed their work, we set fieldstones to provide a sound, level surface for a teak bench (7.3).

Use Paths to Begin a Design

WITH ARBOR AND PAVING in place, we designed a classic four-quadrant herb garden just off the arbor, again using the shed for clues as to its dimensions so that it, the arbor, and the garden would be in harmony. The outer edges of the four beds would be parallel with the two ends of the shed; each bed would be roughly the size of the shed's only door; and the central north-south path as well as the one between the arbor and the first pair of beds would be 6 feet wide—half the width of the shed. The subordinate east-west paths would be one-third of the shed's width, or 4 feet (7.1).

Create Enclosure

WE LAID OUT these dimensions with strings tied to bamboo stakes, then sat under the arbor to look at what we had done. Mary looked north toward the house and barn, only to see that the two north uprights framed a lovely view of our car parked in the barn. We wanted to sit in a little enclosed garden without seeing house, barn, or even the neighbors to the east, and that realization gave rise to an enclosing hedge.

I had just finished reading plantsman Harrison Flint's article in *Horticulture* magazine on unusual hedges and been struck by his recommendation to consider *Viburnum prunifolium*. It has shiny, leathery leaves throughout the growing season, white flowers in May, black berries for birds in late summer, and burgundy red leaves in October (pages 152–53: 1, 2). Two shearings a season maintain its shape.

We laid out the lines of the two hedges. With the 8-foot height of the shed walls in mind, we planted the hedges 10 feet from the ends of the shed. When the hedge was mature, we would have a wide gap between hedge and shed for garden as well as the path leading into the Herb Garden (7.6 and 7.8). We made every straight line in this garden parallel or perpendicular to the fronts and sides of the shed to accent the relationship between building and garden.

We also left two gaps in the hedges that would line up with the central north-south cross path through the garden (7.4). The gap in the south hedge framed a view of the steps leading up onto the shady Rock Garden. At that stage in the development of the Herb Garden, we left its east end open to view a peony and hardy geranium bed we had in mind (7.5). The following spring, we planted the two viburnum hedges using shrubs that were 5 to 6 feet tall.

Seasons Around the Garden Shed:

1. SEPTEMBER *Off the gable end of the garden shed.* 2. LATE OCTOBER *Off the gable end.*
3. SPRING *Off the northwest corner of the garden shed.*   4. WINTER *Off the northwest corner of the garden shed.*

Paths Suggest Their Own Materials

AFTER WE LAID OUT the four quadrants and hedges with string, we removed the sod where the four beds and two hedges would go. We used a straight-nosed spade that had been my grandmother's when she was gardening at her home in Oyster Bay, Long Island. The remaining lawn became paths. Having added sand and compost to the soil, we planted 6-inch-high rooted cuttings of *Buxus koreana* that we had purchased from Ruth Joly at Windsor Road Gardens in Cornish, New Hampshire. Ruth was an old friend of Howard Andros's. We knew we had chosen the right boxwood for the job when we got out of the car at Ruth's nursery to be struck by the extraordinary scent of a 5-foot-high *Buxus koreana* in her entrance garden; it happened to be in full bloom that late April day.

Not many months later, after edging those narrow lawn paths around the four quadrants at least every two weeks to keep grass out of the beds, I realized that, as sumptuous as the lawn paths looked, I didn't have time to keep them perfectly edged.

We took up all the grass and an inch or so of topsoil around all four quadrants, then laid down permeable woven black plastic landscape fabric and covered it with an inch of 3/8-inch pea stone; that solved the maintenance problem. Furthermore, because all the paths outside the Herb Garden were lawn, when we stepped from grass onto pea stone, just as we did in the Beech Tunnel, this small light beige material crunched underfoot, announcing arrival in this new space through both sound and color contrast.

Structure Suggests Plants

ONCE THE LITTLE boxwood hedges were in place and the four beds were ready for planting, we decided to mark the center of each quadrant with a distinctive woody plant. Sometimes design decisions get made on paper and sometimes when browsing in a nursery. We were at Rocky Dale Nursery in Bristol, Vermont, one day looking at what Bill Pollard and Holly Weir had in stock, and discovered the weeping pea shrub (*Caragana arborescens* 'Pendula') on a straight 4-foot-high standard stem; this beautiful yet rugged woody plant blooms with pendulous yellow flowers in late May, and for the rest of the year looks like an oversized

7.4 (opposite) JUNE
Many elements sweep you into the Herb Garden: the mystery of what might be inside those hedges; the wide open gates; the central armillary sphere; the view out the south gateway.

7.5 (overleaf) JUNE
The garden changes from area to area, but always, there in the background, is the reassuring meadow that provides the Ranneys with 1,000 bales of hay each summer.

umbrella. We bought one for the center of each quadrant, where they remain in scale from pruning each season (7.1).

Our shed and arbor also gave us ideas for plants. Near the shed's north entrance we planted a shade-tolerant climbing hydrangea (*Hydrangea petiolaris*) to take advantage of the shed's vertical sides as a display surface for this remarkable clinging vine (7.6). We planted a Van Buren grape vine at the base of one of the arbor's front uprights (7.6) and an Aurora grape on the other front upright. On one of the back uprights we planted a pink-blooming *Clematis* 'Nelly Moser' and a fall-blooming clematis (*Clematis paniculata*) on the fourth post.

Off the west side of the shed, we planted a Royalty crab apple (*Malus* 'Royalty'), with its deep red flowers and leaves, and underplanted it with massed *Geranium macrorrhizum* 'Spessart', which has fragrant evergreen leaves and blooms pink just after the crab apple completes its bloom (7.16). (One of these days we will replace this 'Royalty', because it is utterly vulnerable to scab. We do not use

7.6 JUNE *Even in the Herb Garden, we keep views to nearby gardens open so that the experience of being within the hedges is intimate, not claustrophobic.*

any fungicides—or any chemicals—in the garden, so by the middle of August this crab apple is often almost defoliated.)

We also took advantage of the fact that the two little gardens off either end of the arbor could hold invasive plants at bay. In these areas, bounded by the shed, the stone paving under the arbor, and the ground cloth/pea-stone paths, we planted bee balm (*Monarda* 'Gardenview Scarlet') off the north end of the arbor and coral plume poppy (*Macleaya cordata*) (7.7) interplanted with Oriental lilies off the south end.

Gates Are Gratifying

ONCE WE HAD SHORN the hedges into 8-foot-high, 24-inch-thick hedges, we thought how pleasing gates would look as we entered the Herb Garden from either the north and south gaps in the hedges or from near the front or back of the shed. There's nothing quite like walking up to a gate, lifting a latch, and swinging the gate to enter a space.

We went back to the Hayloft Art Gallery in West Dover and found that the Levines had a pair of unusual gates with scalloped metalwork and three turned wooden spools in the center of each gate (7.4). Jerry Levine told us that they had been crafted in the 1920s by a metalsmith from Georgia; Jerry had bought them from a reclamation shop in New York City where he learned that they had been part of the clerk's entrance to the headquarters of that city's Horn and Hardart Company. (Remember automats, when you put a quarter in a slot, opened a little glass door, and pulled out a plate holding a piece of Boston cream pie?) Anyway, we hung this double gate on black locust posts that now form the north entrance to the Herb Garden.

Andre Bernier visited the garden a few weeks later, saw what we were doing, and said he had a matched pair of gray granite fence posts 5 inches square and 5 feet long that he had gotten on Martha's Vineyard, off the coast of Massachusetts. He brought them over one day and pointed out to us how a white 1/2-inch wide line of quartz ran through both stones on a diagonal from top to bottom. The stones now stand at the two ends of the hedge at the south side of the Herb Garden (7.9).

7.7 SUMMER *A solid locust post stands in contrast to the leaves and stem of coral plume poppy (*Macleaya cordata*).*

With entrances marked both north and south, we knew we needed gates for the two west entrances. We conferred with Ian Eddy, a blacksmith in nearby Putney, Vermont, on the design of two black wrought-iron gates; they now hang on black locust posts at either end of the shed (7.8).

A Garden Needs a Center

THE PLACE where the two central paths intersected is literally the center of the Herb Garden. To mark that spot, to mark any center, is an important anchoring gesture we always try to make. We bought an armillary sphere (a form of sundial) and a finely cast English pedestal from Dieta Matthiesen, near Cambridge, New York, and set the pedestal at the meeting point of the two main paths. The moment we set the armillary sphere on it and three germander (*Teucrium chamaedrys*) around its base, we felt we had made a good decision (7.9).

This refined pair of ornaments marks the center of this formally organized but informally planted herb garden, and provides just that lift of tone and hint of refinement that makes them stand in pleasing contrast to the old garden shed.

The visual role these ornaments play is important when we're *in* the garden as well as walking toward it. When standing on the mossy steps in the Rock Garden looking north into the Herb Garden, for example, or when walking south from the barn, the sphere and pedestal capture our attention and hold it until we are actually in the Herb Garden. Were these ornaments not there or not visually strong enough, our attention would slide right down the length of the central pea-stone path and out the north or south gaps in the hedge. The center holds our eye.

7.8 (opposite) JULY
Many things say "Enter": the stepping-stones and the pot to their right; the open gate; the promise of detail in the wheelbarrow and the planted pots in the distance.

7.9 (below) AUGUST
Gardens need strong visual centers. Here we used an English armillary sphere to form a center around which all parts gather.

7.10 *(opposite)* AUGUST
This is a concrete cast of The Green Woman, *the original of which was carved in stone for The Cathedral of St. John the Divine in New York City by Jessica Aujero, a journeyman stone carver. This cast sculpture hangs next to the door into our garden shed. (Door latch by Scott Bolotin.)*

7.11 *(below)* AUGUST
This fiberglass cast from Design Toscano was taken from an original nineteenth-century Siennese terra-cotta plaque of Vappa, a minor Roman deity related to wine.

Decorate Walls of Buildings

THE TEXTURE AND COLOR of the weathered wooden siding on the shed turned out to be a suitable background for two plaques. Ever since Gerry Prozzo carved the Green Man into the butternut stump in the Dining Area, we had been on the lookout for Green Men sculptures or plaques to add to the garden. One day at our friend Allison McRae's garden shop in Brattleboro, Mary spotted a sand cast of *The Green Woman*, a modern take on this ancient symbol. Because it looked old, we set it just to the left of the garden shed door as a spirit of entry (7.10). We also hung a white fiberglass bas-relief of Vappa (7.11) on the east wall of the shed. Bunches of grapes are woven into her hair; Van Buren grapes grow on the arbor deck above her, so when the grapes are ripening, they provide an echo of those in Vappa's hair.

The Many Roles of Hedges

ABOUT THREE YEARS after we had planted the *Viburnum prunifolium* hedges to enclose the north and south sides of the Herb Garden, we thought it was time to enclose the east end. We planted fifteen emerald green arborvitae (*Thuja occidentalis* 'Smaragd'), knowing that this evergreen hedge would play at least four roles in the garden (7.1). First, it completes the enclosure of the Herb Garden, thereby more clearly defining its meaning; without the hedge, the feeling of the garden was leaking out the east gap. Second, it screens views, albeit distant, of neighbors' houses and cars when we are sitting on the bench. Third, it separates the Herb Garden from the peony and geranium bed, which we planted adjacent to the east edge of the Herb Garden (7.5), while at the same time providing the peony and geranium bed with a uniformly green background. Fourth, it acts as a backdrop for a plan we had for herbs in terra-cotta pots.

We ordered thirty-six 22-inch-high but only 8-inch-wide Long Tom terra-cotta pots with an eye to planting a single tender herb in each. In this way we grow unusual heat- and drought-tolerant herbs for the kitchen, and display the line of pots along the length of the evergreen hedge. We give this line a center with a 3-foot-high terra-cotta rhubarb-forcing pot from Whichford Pottery in

England (7.12). (Our cottage and garden in England, the subject of Chapter 10, is only 10 miles from Whichford Pottery, so there was an echo of the England we know in this tall terra-cotta ornament.)

We also found that the ends of the *Viburnum prunifolium* hedges formed an appropriate backdrop for large planted terra-cotta pots (7.8 and 7.14). Each year, we place 24-inch-diameter terra-cotta pots off the west end of each viburnum hedge around Memorial Day and plant them with richly colored annuals to attract attention to the entrances to the Herb Garden.

By using only terra-cotta pots, we take advantage of the important design principle of *theme and variation*. Introducing into this small garden area pots of varying materials—fiberglass, glazed ceramic, cast stone, plastic—would have created a potentially busy, unsettled look, one that would confirm we weren't sure in which direction to take the garden. By choosing terra-cotta as our theme, and varying that with Long Toms, a rhubarb forcer, and the large pots at the end of the hedges, we create variety within restraint. The result is coherence and clarity.

The visually strong 35-foot-long, 8-foot-high *Viburnum prunifolium* hedges can be seen from almost anywhere in the garden. These large green geometric blocks stand in pleasing contrast to all the other free-flowing forms as well as colors of shrubs and trees throughout the garden, while also acting as a visual reference point against which to measure the freer forms of unsheared trees, shrubs, and perennials (7.14 and 7.15). At the same time, the hedges act as a living echo of the geometry of the nearby shed, house, and gazebo. These architectural hedges, then, act not only as backdrops for plants within the Herb Garden but outside it as well. When coming up the central lawn in the Long Borders, for example, we see part of the viburnum hedge in the background stand in pleasing contrast to the frilly and evergreen *Chamaecyparis pisifera 'Filifera'* hedge in the foreground. When we stand among the crab apples in the Orchard looking toward the Herb Garden, we see the shapes and forms created by their branching, foliage, and red fruit stand out against the strong geometric hedge. These hedges are solid, virtually unchanging objects

7.12 *(opposite)* AUGUST
Under the branches of a weeping pea shrub you can see a rhubarb forcing pot from Whichford Pottery in England.

7.13 *(below)* MAY
Dicentra formosa *and a young peony grow next to the small Long Tom pots we line up at the bottom of the herb garden each year.*

7.14 *(opposite)* JULY
The dense Viburnum prunifolium *hedge combines with the south side of the shed to create strong geometric forms against which to appreciate the organic forms of the silver willow and* Malus *'Royalty'.*

7.15 *(below)* SEPTEMBER
Magnolia *'Miss Honey Bee' with its huge light green leaves stands in pleasing contrast to the geometric dark green viburnum hedge. Foreground and background help each other.*

(because we shear them) against which to take the measure of other areas of the garden.

Mark the Ends of Long, Straight Paths

WE OFTEN MARK the ends of straight paths with a garden ornament: to draw attention down the length of a path, to create a visual conclusion at the end of a sight line, to clearly define depth and distance, and to emphasize a mood. All these reasons explain why we have the old wheelbarrow that our friend Woody Fuller made for us at the end of the south path into the Herb Garden. As we enter the iron gate off the southwest corner of the garden shed, and even as we step down the last of the steps in the Entry Garden, we look east and see right through the iron gates to the old wheelbarrow at the end of the pea-stone path in the Herb Garden (7.8). The wheelbarrow stops our eye and holds it.

As we were about to plant the south *Viburnum prunifolium* hedge, we had to decide whether to cut down the mature rock maple growing close to the southeast corner of the Herb Garden. If we wanted a thriving hedge and a sunny herb garden, the maple had to go. Over the years we had gradually removed twenty or so smaller maples from that area to let sun into the sun-loving Herb Garden, but now it was crunch time for the big tree.

Rather than cut it down to the ground, I cut it about 18 feet aboveground and girdled the base of the trunk with a chain saw to prevent it from sending up sprouts. We're training the robust *Rosa* 'William Baffin' up the trunk.

7.16 *(overleaf)* MAY *We are blessed to have this old shed at the heart of our garden. It adds a deep sense of time past to our new garden.*

Big Views, Small Places

WHEN WE LEAVE the seclusion and enclosure of our Herb Garden, we see a broad view from all four entrances: a 30-acre meadow and distant ridgelines of hills to the south and east; the broad lawn and orchard to the west; and the lawn panel along the west side of the Spring Garden, with a view to the gardens to the north and the Ranneys' barn in the distance. By taking advantage of the frames created by gaps in hedges and by gateways, we focus attention on a big view from a small place (7.1), and we take a lot of pleasure from that.

Two Seasons in the Herb Garden

1. SUMMER *Grapes abound, the alliums are in bloom, the variegated horseradish is thriving.*

2. WINTER *All has gone quiet; only arborvitae and boxwood, leafless peashrubs, locust wood, and snow remain to tell the story.*

8

The Spring Garden

IN MID-MARCH 1984, we spotted the first thawed ground to appear since we had moved in the previous December. We were on it immediately. In the copse of wild plums, we pulled weeds from the wet soil, picked up dead branches, cut down maple saplings that were growing straight up through the contorted black trunks of the plums, and pruned the tangle of dead lower branches. It was magic to be working under that canopy after a winter in the house.

Trees Suggest Bed Edges

WE WANTED TO MAKE A GARDEN under these wild plum trees, but as always we had to work out its limits first. The east edge of this moist area in filtered shade was established by our property line, but what clues were there to help us with the other three edges so the garden would feel right and inevitable in its place? The drip line of the copse gave us the clue we needed to the west and south. With a straight-nosed spade, I cut a long, dropped edge that roughly followed the outermost tips of the branches along the entire south and west sides of the copse. The result was a broad, sweeping, curved edge where bed met lawn. (By 2001, at which point several wild plums at the edge had died, the old logic gave way to a new one, but more on that below.) The north edge of this new bed took care of itself among small maple trees underplanted with dead nettle and hostas. That was easy.

8.1 *(opposite)* EARLY MAY *Wild plums form a fragrant, uniform white canopy over all the colors of our Spring Garden. A simple bridge invites guests into this wild copse.*

8.2 *(overleaf)* EARLY MAY *For three weeks, our Spring Garden is an unruly, ethereal place.*

Paths and Bridges

WITH EDGES CLARIFIED, we looked to the interior of the space under the wild plums for clues as to where to put the path through it. *Good paths have lots of prepositions*; we wanted to walk *off* lawn and *onto* a new material at either end of the path, walk *through* the full length of the garden, *under* the canopy of branches, and *among* and *between* the contorted trunks of the trees. We looked for pairs of trees and view lines between them to help establish the two ends of the path. We looked for the most interesting contorted trunks to flank the path. Once we had the two entrances and the points of interest along the way, we joined them with stepping-stones (8.2).

But there was one intriguing 6-foot-wide dip in the ground along the south end of the path. One of the seven generations of farmers who preceded us must have dug this shallow trench to drain water from what had been the small barn we dismantled. Given that clue as to the possible purpose of the ditch, we didn't fill it but built an 8-foot-long simple wooden bridge across it (8.1). By quietly introducing a new material into the garden, this wooden bridge emphasizes this particular vantage point in the Spring Garden. It also adds the mystery and sense of passage that any bridge carries.

Flowers Above, Flowers Below

BY THE TIME we finished all this preparatory work in mid-April, the entire canopy of plum trees was in full bloom (page 176). Those sweetly scented white flowers gave us the idea to plant perennials and shrubs under the plums that would bloom around the same time as the trees: white above; yellows, pinks, purples, whites, and blues below. That is, we wanted to create simultaneous bloom in the trees above and in the shrubs and perennials below.

Because this was a naturalistic area with a relaxed structure established only by copse and path, we did not need to turn to structure plants in the way we had in the Brick Walk Garden and the Long Borders. Here we could mass perennials and individual specimens to our hearts' content and the garden would hold together visually. In fact, we didn't even follow our rule of choos-

Two Seasons in the Spring Garden

1. SPRING *A Thai pot and the curvy boxwood hedge create a threshold to draw guests into our Spring Garden at the peak of its bloom.*

2. AUTUMN *The south entrance is much quieter in autumn, with maple foliage providing a flash.*

ing shrubs first, then perennials. We thought out the variables that drove plant choice, then planted whatever appealed to us.

- Bloom anytime from April into mid-May
- Thrive in filtered shade
- Grow well in moist but heavy soil
- Flourish in Zone 4 (-20° to -25° Fahrenheit)
- Look good the rest of the year

Some of the first plants we put in were shrubs along the back of the garden to screen us from our neighbor's house: *Viburnum sargentii* 'Onondaga'; *Rhododendron mucronulatum*, with its clear pink flowers; and *Pieris japonica* 'Mountain Fire', among others. In a tip of the hat to Alice Holway, who had always wanted a primrose path, we planted lots and lots of *Primula veris* (Alice gave us the starter plants) and *P. denticulata* (8.3). One early September day two years later, Howard Andros arrived with an envelope of seeds he had selected from burgundy or strong pink candelabra primroses (*Primula japonica*) growing in his garden. We scattered Howard's seeds that September throughout the Spring Garden and lightly raked them in. Two springs later, candelabras were everywhere.

We also planted white bleeding-heart (*Lamprocapnos spectabilis* 'Alba'), the fast-spreading *Epimedium* 'Sulphureum', and the slower spreading *E.* x *rubrum* and *E.* 'White Queen', among many other spring-blooming perennials. Over the years we added plants that bloom at the other end of the gardening year, especially rodgersias and ligularias, to bring more interest to this area not only in flower but in huge, lasting foliage (8.4). But what lasts for the entire calendar year are the black trunks and tangled branches of the wild plums, which even in the dead of winter create an untamed feeling in the garden.

Lawn Paths Link Beds

TO ESTABLISH THE EDGE of the Spring Garden, we followed its drip line, creating a curvilinear bed and lawn edge. To establish the nearby east edge of the Herb Garden, we cut straight edges to follow the logic of this linear garden. The awkwardly

8.3 MAY *The contorted trunks and rough branching of the wild plums stand in contrast to delicate daffodils, primulas, pulmonarias, and the Cornell Pink azalea to the left.*

shaped lawn that resulted between curve and straight made little sense. It was neither a path nor a well-conceived shape. It didn't help to pull the two gardens on either side of it into a relationship with each other; in fact, it said loud and clear: "The beds on either side of me are not related."

We needed a bridge, a transition lawn that would let us create a uniformly wide lawn path between the two. What we did made all the difference to those two gardens.

The curvy west edge of the Spring Garden provided the better line for a lawn path to follow than did the straight east edge of the Herb Garden. The curve would add mystery because its destination was ambiguous, and enable us to break the linearity dictated by the garden shed and Herb Garden. I measured 6 feet to the west of the curvy edge along the Spring Garden, inserted bamboo

8.4 MAY *This uniformly 5-foot-wide curving lawn path follows the dripline of the wild plum copse—its curve is logical and feels right.*

stakes, then removed all the lawn outside the stakes to make a uniform 6-foot-wide lawn path (8.4). This lawn now had a logical shape, and it let the two gardens on either side of it relate to each other. To fill the area where the lawn had been, we extended the peony and geranium bed (7.5).

Low Hedges, High Hedges

Y EARS LATER we strengthened the line of that curvilinear lawn path with a low hedge of Hicks yew (*Taxus* x *media* 'Hicksii') that extended the line of the lawn path around to the south entrance of the Herb Garden. To increase the feeling of entry into the Spring Garden, we added a low boxwood hedge (*Buxus microphylla* 'Green Mountain') to the left of the entrance (8.4). As with all evergreens, these yew and boxwood hedges, in combination

8.5 AUGUST 2002
Large-leaved ligularias, brunneras, *and* rodgersias *carry the Spring Garden into late summer.*

A Year in the Development of a New Area, 2003: 1. APRIL *We took up excess lawn to create a straight-edged panel of lawn, and then set stepping-stones.* 2. JUNE *We planted the hedge and new perennials to link the new area to the existing Spring Garden.*

3. AUTUMN

Autumn in the
new area.

4. WINTER

The new rectangle
of lawn is especially
clear between new
and existing hedges.

with the arborvitae hedge running north-south at the bottom of the Herb Garden, became essential elements in the look of our winter garden.

To give the area due west of the main body of the Spring Garden even more form and to separate it from the driveway, we planted a 24-inch-high yew hedge (*Taxus* x *media* 'Hicksii') from the north gap in the *Viburnum prunifolium* hedge to the southeast corner of the barn (8.6), leaving two gaps marked with black locust posts for access to the north part of the garden as well as the Spring Garden. As we allowed that hedge to grow 5 feet high, it shifted a balance in the garden: the taller the hedge, the more powerful its presence. Being geometric, tightly sheared, and dark green, it made ever-increasing demands to be more than just a screen. It became a force to be reckoned with. And it, along with other alterations, eventually drove a major change in the shape of the lawn and bed in this area.

Time Creates Changes

OVER THE YEARS, many of the wild plums at the edge of the northern two-thirds of the Spring Garden died, therefore compromising that drip line as the reason for the curvy lawn. This area of lawn was one of the weak points in the design of the garden because it did not pull together the straight hedge and the curvy bed into a coherent whole. In fact, by its odd shape, it separated areas and broke down relationships (pages 182–83).

Several other garden elements in this area had changed as well, all of which caused us to rethink the shape of this lawn.

■ To anchor this oddly shaped lawn, we had planted a crab apple (*Malus* 'Donald Wyman') about 17 feet east of the center of the yew hedge; it had matured into a lovely small tree, but it was a temporary solution to a design problem.

■ In the past fifteen years or so, we had developed a new entrance to the gardens to the north of the barn. To the east of the entrance was a 20-foot-long, 7-foot-high emerald green arborvitae hedge; to the west was a 20-foot-high amur maple (*Acer tataricum ginnala*) (8.6).

■ We had developed the north area beyond the new entrance to such a degree that it was now as important as the Herb Garden. Furthermore, we could now see various elements of that new garden when standing in the north gap in the Herb Garden. Visual weight had shifted and was asking this oddly shaped lawn to confirm that view, but it wasn't up to the task.

Taking into account all these changes, in the spring of 2002 we addressed the problem of the badly shaped lawn. It clearly needed to become a rectangular panel of lawn that would pull the north exit from the Herb Garden and the south entrance to the Dell and the other North Gardens into a stronger relationship with one another. We measured the distance from the east side of the 5-foot-high yew hedge and found that leaving a 16-foot-wide straight panel of lawn between the Herb Garden and the Dell, and removing the rest of the lawn between it and the west edge of the Spring Garden, would create several new elements of coherence.

By removing all the grass from the east edge of this new panel of lawn, we could extend the Spring Garden. The Donald Wyman crab apple would be 1 foot into this new bed and form an anchor for it as well (pages 182–83). By choosing the 16-foot dimension, the east edge of the new lawn panel lined up exactly with the arborvitae hedge at the bottom of the Herb Garden. To further support that line, we planted another Hicks yew hedge parallel with and 17 feet from the existing yew hedge, thereby framing the panel of lawn with yew hedges to draw an even stronger relationship between the Herb Garden and the Dell (page 186).

Old Paths to New Areas

BEFORE PLANTING the new yew hedge, we had to decide how to extend the existing stepping-stone paths into this new garden area. The existing *Malus* 'Donald Wyman' gave us the clue. By adding a Y-shaped extension to the existing north end of the path through the Spring Garden, we could give this lovely crab apple new significance. This Y-shaped path also gave us a perfect new spot for an important garden ornament, one that has a story behind it (8.7).

The new geometric panel of lawn answers the straight hedges and frames a view from the Herb Garden to the North Gardens.

Ornaments with Emotion

ON THE FIRST OF TWO TRIPS I made to England with Peter and Theodora Berg in the late 1980s, Peter purchased, among many other garden ornaments, several antique staddle stones and had them shipped to their garden in New Hampshire. As we unloaded the shipping container, Theodora gave me one of the staddle stones to give to Mary for our garden.

The English staddle stone is an agricultural artifact. Before the advent of the combine harvester, Mary's father set eighteen or so of these in a 16-foot-diameter circle, placed planks across their tops, then stacked bound sheaves of wheat atop this raised platform to store and dry them in what was called the rickyard. The staddle stone's overhang discouraged rats and mice from climbing into the valuable grain. In placing this garden ornament in our

Changing Bed/ Lawn Shapes

1. SPRING 2003 *The lawn was in the shape of a grand piano. Such a shape did not relate beds adjacent to it but separated them.*

2. MID-SUMMER 2003 *After giving a shape to an amorphous lawn, we planted a new yew hedge parallel to the existing one, pulling two previously unrelated areas together.*

8.7 *(previous page)* JUNE *Mary's father used staddle stones like this one on his farm when Mary was growing up. The round base of this staddle stone tells us it is from East Sussex.*

8.8 *(above)* MAY *The P.J.M. Rhododendron has become a cliché in American gardening, but cliché or not, it sure is strutting its stuff here.*

garden at the Y in this important new path, we strengthened our Old England–New England connection.

This ornament serves several other purposes: with the crab apple tree, it anchors this new part of the garden; and it provides a visual destination for the path; and it supports a logic, with the crab apple tree, for why the path splits just there.

Given all these changes, this strong panel of lawn supported by two yew hedges creates much stronger coherence. The Herb Garden and the Dell, previously unrelated, are drawn into a stronger visual relationship; the two yew hedges relate to each other through their shared line, form, and material; the crab apple tree now has a context that it previously lacked; and the faltering logic of the drip line was replaced with a new logic of the straight line. Parts pulled together to form a whole.

9

The North Gardens

THE STRUCTURE FOR THE GARDENS to the north of the house and barn arose naturally from the abandoned stone barn foundations (T, U, V, W on map), but this ease of design came at a price. The amount of cleanup we had to do in this area was remarkable. Shoveling into what looked like deep, rich leaf mold in one area, we found that 2 inches of beautifully decomposed leaves were in fact sitting atop 2 feet of broken-down asphalt shingles interspersed with rusting metal roofing panels and scrap metal. We dug and hauled for two days before reaching soil riddled with nails, broken glass, pail handles, rusted cans, and maple sap buckets. The rest of the area was not all that different. This was turning into farm archaeology.

The Pool Garden

ONE DAY when we were clearing the area, Mary's rake hit concrete. We scraped and raked and shoveled twenty years or more of decayed leaves, sticks, brambles, and two maple saplings that had taken root in the leaf mold before uncovering a cracked 18-foot-diameter concrete base of a silo. We swept it off and hosed it down. A few days later, we realized that it would make the perfect base for a pool there under the ash trees. We covered the concrete with 2 inches of sand, spread a butyl rubber liner over it, then covered the liner with 2 inches of pea stone to hide the liner. Knowing that what the locals call "ginger stone" wicks up water that gives rise to a thick layer of bright green moss and ferns on the rock, we ringed the pool (and held the outer edge of

9.1 MAY *Stones are the bones of heaven and earth . . . and our pool garden. Water, stone's opposite, brings those bones alive.*

the liner down) with these lightweight, pumicey dark brown stones, making sure that their bases were in the water. We then intermixed those ginger stones with gray granite boulders, which would give rise to gray lichens. Those stones are now little gardens in themselves that the frogs sit on during summer days (9.1).

Knowing that we wanted sparkling, not still, water in this pool, we turned to the history of the place for inspiration as to how to create a small fountain or bubbler in its center. What would the Ranneys have had or made generations ago that water passed through? Then it hit us: an old granite or marble wellhead. Colonists had set one of these circular 6- to 8-inch thick, 5-foot-diameter stones with a hole cut in its center atop a stone-lined dug well. They passed a pipe through the hole and into the water below, then affixed a hand pump to the pipe and wellhead for their water supply.

Local antiques dealer Gene Bourne told me that his uncle, Cecil Buffam, over in West Rupert, Vermont, had a 200-year-old Danby marble wellhead for sale. I drove the hour across the state, and Cecil loaded this magnificent stone into my pickup with his bulldozer.

I had arranged for Ellis Derrig to have his backhoe ready for my return. He lowered the wellhead onto four 8-inch-thick stones that I had set on the bottom of the pool to hold it off the rubber liner. I hid a pump under the central hole in the wellhead and plugged it in. After some adjustment, we succeeded in having an 8-inch white mound of water come above the surface of the stone (9.1).

Standing Stones Mark Entrances

JUST AS WITH the stepping-stone path in the Woodland Garden, we wanted to mark the beginning of the stepping-stone path that started by the pool and went east into gardens within the old barn foundation. Stepping-stones, especially when surrounded by plants, are not obvious to people new to the garden. By sheer chance, stonemason Andre Bernier, who had done a lot of work for us over the years, called and said he had a long, narrow stone for our new garden. He suggested we put a red flag in the ground near

9.2 MAY *The standing stone announces there is something important going on over there. Stepping-stones set within* Sedum *'Dr. John Creech' and yellow-leaved creeping Jenny show the way.*

where we'd install it and he'd deliver it when he had a chance. I put the red flag in the lawn near the pool. A week or so later when we were walking around the garden, as we do every late afternoon, we saw Andre's stone: 10 feet long, 2 feet wide, and a foot thick. I called to thank him for the stone and ask how he had delivered it. He had cut several old broom handles into 3-foot lengths and set them on the bed of his pickup. He lowered the stone with straps and chains with the front loader of a tractor, then tied the stone to the bed of his truck. When he got to our place, he untied the ropes and then, in reverse, gunned it. Ten feet from the red flag he hit the brakes, and the stone rolled off the broom handles and thumped to the ground.

I called Ellis Derrig again; he sent Bill Fitzpatrick up with the backhoe. Bill dug a 3-foot-deep hole and, with hefty nylon straps, set the stone on end into the ground. The stepping-stone path now starts in the gap between the pool edge and the standing stone (9.1), then runs east through and arrives at the next major section of the garden, the Milking Parlor, within the barn foundation.

Existing Edges Help

WE SET ABOUT DESIGNING the 20-foot-wide space between the pool and the concrete base of the old milking parlor some 30 feet to the east (W on map). The existing edges were right there in front of us: the pool to the west, the stone foundation wall to the south, the raised concrete milking parlor to the east, and the dirt road to the north (1.11).

To reinforce the north edge and screen us from the frequently traveled dirt road (I have to admit, "frequently traveled" on this particular Vermont road means six cars an hour during rush hour), we planted a row of eighteen emerald green arborvitae (*Thuja occidentalis* 'Smaragd') along the north edge of the Pool Garden. To strengthen the west edge, to provide a background for the pool, and to screen it from the nearby road, we planted six Miss Kim lilacs (*Syringa patula* 'Miss Kim').

To reinforce the south edge, initially marked only by a 16-inch-high stone wall, we set five vertical black locust posts along the length of the stone wall, then attached pairs of rusty chain swags

9.3 *(above)* OCTOBER
Even as members of the Anglican and Congregational churches, Mary and I enjoy the peace of the Buddha, a fact that amuses our Buddhist friend and neighbor Waew Kasetrevatin.

9.4 *(opposite)* AUTUMN
*Kuma bamboo grass (*Sasa veitchii*) conjures a quiet Asian quote, and complements Buddha.*

between each pair of posts and planted a male and female variegated kiwi vine (*Actinidia kolomikta*), which we tied to the chains. This semitransparent screen now separates the Dell to the south and the Pool Garden to the north and provides us with edible kiwi fruit (9.11). Without that suggestion of a screen, the separate purposes of the two adjacent gardens would have remained muddied.

With pool and edges established, we turned our attention to the interior of the space. Given that one of the primary reasons to garden is to get in among, to see, smell, and touch plants, we looked for clues as to where a path should run to get us among the plants, not just past them. The decision made itself. The space between the pool and the mammoth standing stone now forms the west entrance to the path. The east entrance is a low spot in the concrete/stone raised milking parlor that needed only one flat stone step to help us get up onto the Milking Parlor. By connecting these areas with a broadly curving stepping-stone path, we created the spine of the garden, a sound starting point for plant selection.

Plants for Different Purposes

WHEN IT COMES to choosing plants, we start with the big and work toward the small, but we also look to plants to solve specific problems. Power lines across the road compromised the area's calm feeling, so we planted a cork tree (*Phellodendron amurense*) that friend and fellow garden designer Christian Fenderson had given us. This magnificent tree now spreads its branches over both pool and path. And because I have been high-pruning it, the arborvitae hedge under it receives enough light to stay dense and attractive.

We then planted several *Fothergilla gardenii* on either side of the central path to provide a repeated form down the length of the garden. These shrubs provide flowers in May, witch-hazel-like foliage through the summer, and remarkable color in the fall. We planted a pair of Hicks yews (*Taxus* x *media* 'Hicksii') at the center back of the pool that now hold the eye. We marked the entrance to the Milking Parlor with a globe arborvitae.

We then surrounded the pool with low perennials, so as not to obscure the view. To visually link pool to path, we repeated certain

plants along its length: *Ajuga reptans* 'Gaiety', with its burgundy red leaves, European ginger (*Asarum europaeum*), and woodland and creeping phlox transplants from the Woodland Garden. Today, taller, moisture-tolerant perennials grow there as well: astilbes, hostas, ferns, the pink-flowering fall anemone (*Anemone tomentosa* 'Robustissima'), and the variegated bamboo *Sasa veitchii* (9.4).

We also wanted to mass a broad-leaved perennial in this area to contrast with the many frilly leaved plants. The first year, we planted butterburr (*Petasites japonicus*) in this area, much against Mary's wishes. I loved the leaves, which could get as much as 2 feet across; she was concerned about how invasive the plant is. She was right. We removed every plant we put in, but after three years it

9.5 SUMMER *These chairs, just outside the north door of our barn, offer us a peaceful, cool place to sit after a day of work.*

9.6 JUNE *The Milking Parlor gives us a raised vantage point from which to look back at the garden.*

had already run into, as well as under, the stone wall, within the dense roots of the maple tree, and under the concrete of the Milking Parlor. Even now we still battle it.

Next, we tried purple-leaved rhubarb (*Rheum palmatum* 'Atrosanguineum'), and ran afoul of the vagaries of nature. It looked terrific the first year, dry as it was. The following year was very rainy, and we lost all but two we had planted in the upper, drier area of the garden, and even they didn't look good. This past fall, Fred McGourty, who retired years ago from the Brooklyn Botanic Garden, and his wife, Maryanne, visited the garden from their home in Norfolk, Connecticut. Fred suggested we replace the rhubarb with a new ligularia he had just seen: *Ligularia dentata* 'Britt Marie Crawford', with its 18-inch-wide burgundy red leaves on plants that will grow to 3 feet high or more. It's listed as a Zone 5 plant, a bit warmer than we are, but we're going to try it.

Where Plants Won't Grow

NOW WE HAD to decide what to do with the undeveloped area between the northeast end of the barn and the pool. For years we had called some combination of weeds and grass a lawn, but we were in denial. It was a weed patch. It was in the complete shade of three trees that used to be much smaller. Furthermore, these three—a sugar maple, an ash, and a Japanese tree lilac (*Syringa reticulata*)—are difficult to garden under because their aggressive root systems gather in the top 3 feet of ground. We didn't want to remove the trees because they made a lovely grouping and provided shade, scale, and maturity, but we simply couldn't garden under them with any success.

We removed the struggling grass from the area, then laid down permeable woven black plastic landscape fabric and covered it with 2 inches of beige pea stone (9.5). We then set large stones under the ash tree as a base for two armchairs as well as for potted plants. Now we are able to sit there in the shade of the trees and enjoy the calm of the pool, its splashing water, and the garden all around. In making this new sitting area, where we relax virtually every evening of the growing season, we had followed an important principle: make each sitting area in our garden grow out of its

9.7 AUGUST *Milk cans support a sense of place on the steps up to the abandoned milking parlor. The trumpet vine adds a wild hint to the romantic.*

199

site, its existing conditions, and its sense of place. We allow the place to define the nature of the space where we'll sit. In that way, each sitting area has its own qualities, its own nature, feeling, and role in the overall garden; guide nature, don't control it.

Now that we had clarified the edges and the floor of this new sitting area, I looked up. The branches of the two trees closest to the barn—the maple and the ash—were only 8 feet above the ground. I got out my 30-foot extension ladder and cut off all the interior branches from the maple and ash that were directly above the chairs where we would sit. By leaving all exterior branches intact but removing interior ones, I created a 30-foot high open space within these two trees that added immeasurably to the calm, lofty, and peaceful nature of this new sitting area.

The Milking Parlor

J UST AFTER we unearthed the silo base in the summer of 1984, we turned our attention to the raised flat area to the east (V on map), wondering whether it too was concrete. It was. By raking off years of decomposed leaves and sticks, we uncovered a flat area of cracked concrete 8 feet wide and about 25 feet long. It had clearly been shaped to create runnels and places for cows to stand while being milked (9.6 and 9.12).

Rather than remove the concrete, we mixed the well-composted leaf mold we had been collecting with topsoil and sifted it into the runnels and cracks of the flat concrete surface. In it we planted thymes, sedums, and other ground-hugging, drought-tolerant species to create a kind of flat tapestry effect on the ground: *Thymus serpyllum*, *Thymus pseudolanuginosus*, *Delosperma nubigenum*, hens and chicks in variety, *Sedum pachyclados*, and *Thymus citriodorus*, among many others.

The Calf Pen Garden

F OUR FEET BELOW and to the east of the Milking Parlor was an area that Harold Ranney told us was where earlier farmers had built a roofed but otherwise open-air place for calves. Being the lowest corner of this north part of the garden, it collected water and drained poorly, so we didn't run a path through it. What we

9.8 SEPTEMBER
The chartreuse leaves of Hosta *'Sum and Substance' complement the light yellow leaves of* Kirengeshoma palmata *in a shady, moist corner of our North Gardens.*

did do and continue to do is choose moisture-tolerant plants for the area: golden-twigged dogwood (*Cornus stolonifera* 'Flaviramea'), with its bright yellow stems, and *Cornus stolonifera* 'Cardinal', with its remarkable apricot-orange stems in winter, both of which I can see from my office upstairs in the east end of the barn; *Viburnum sargentii* 'Onondaga', *Salix alba vitellina*, *Cornus alba* 'Elegantissima', and, later, in the drier southern edge of this garden, a mass of *Hydrangea paniculata* 'Unique'.

To create a wild look in this far corner of the garden, we underplanted these shrubs with bee balm (*Monarda didyma*); white as well as blue forms of *Iris sibirica*; sweet woodruff (*Galium odoratum*); daylilies; the ground cover yellow archangel (*Lamium galeobdolon* 'Florentinum'), out of which grew culver's root (*Veronicastrum virginicum* 'Album'); and ironweed (*Vernonia glauca*).

A native paper birch is still growing near the southeast corner of the Milking Parlor; we planted an orange-flowering trumpet vine (*Campsis radicans*), a strong-grower that would climb the white trunk (9.7).

The Dell

THE DELL settles into the right angle of the abandoned barn foundation. For years it was a low-sitting, free-form lawn that resembled a huge grand piano. The shape of the lawn bore no relationship to the nearby abandoned barn foundation, the Milking

9.9 *(below, left)* SPRING 2003 *The previous lawn shape in the Dell did not relate to hedges, the east end of the barn, the stone foundation, anything.*

9.10 *(below, right)* ONE DAY LATER *Once we settled on the ellipse as a strong shape for the lawn (see T on the map), we cut away all excess lawn to make this new shape that does relate to all the above.*

9.11 *(overleaf)* JULY *By capturing this view of our neighbor Howard Prussack's barn many hundreds of yards away, we underpin the connection between our North Gardens and their agricultural context.*

Parlor, or the sitting area by the pool; nothing justified its shape, so it looked just plain silly (9.9). We had installed it early in our garden-making, and it stuck. In 2001, we decided to change and clarify its shape by removing lawn at the edges, to leave a strong green geometric shape, one that would hold the center of the Dell and relate to its edges.

All the clues as to lawn shape were there had we heeded them earlier. The first was the stone wall running east-west along the south side of the Pool Garden. The second was the arborvitae hedge at the east edge of the Calf Pen Garden. The third was the east end of the barn and the stone wall that ran north and parallel with another arborvitae hedge parallel with the wall. The only unhelpful edge was on the south, where a small stone wall and an arborvitae hedge went off on a diagonal toward the southeast (9.9).

We found that the existing lawn on the east-west axis was 40 feet

9.12 JUNE *We will maintain the gap between the two arborvitaes that frame a view of the Ranneys' house, but let the evergreen shrubs close all the other gaps so that our intention is clear.*

long. We measured its highly irregular width at various points and found that leaving an 18-foot-wide, 40-foot-long panel of lawn would enable us to remove as little lawn as possible yet create a rectangle, ellipse, or oval with existing lawn. We decided on an ellipse (9.10).

We marked the edges of this new shape with bamboo stakes, then removed the lawn outside them. We added stepping-stones of the same mica schist we had used nearby to link this new ellipse with the Milking Parlor, the Spring Garden, and the Pool Garden. The ellipse now draws the surrounding gardens into a strong relationship with one another (pages 232–33).

Ornaments Emphasize Sense of Place

BY REPLACING the weak bottleneck of lawn between the Spring Garden lawn and the ellipse with large stepping-stones surrounded by plants (9.11), we created a much stronger sense of entrance. As we walk along the newly made rectangle of lawn west of the Spring Garden (between P and T on map), we arrive not at more lawn and an indistinct transition but at a strong change of material underfoot to confirm that we are leaving one garden area and entering another. We strengthened that feeling of entrance with a small cast stone pedestal supporting a small planted terracotta pot. On the other side of the entrance, we balanced the pedestal/pot combination with Winter Flame dogwood (*Cornus sanguinea* 'Winter Flame') (9.11).

Now when we walk through this transition area and step onto the ellipse, we have two choices: go right and up steps onto the Milking Parlor, or go left and up steps to the Pool Garden. Whenever the beginning of two nearby paths appear in one view, we like to make one dominant and the other subordinate. Knowing that if guests took the choice to the left, they would miss seeing the Milking Parlor, we needed to add garden ornaments that would draw attention to the preferred path to the right.

At an antique shop in a barn in northern Vermont one autumn day, we came upon three old rusty milk cans. They were just the thing to put on either side of the steps to the Milking Parlor to add the visual weight we wanted (9.12). After all, the farmers who preceded us would likely have set milk cans on steps very similar to

the ones we had at the south end of the Milking Parlor.

To give some focus to the ellipse, and given that this area is wet much of the year, we planted a small tree form of the white-variegated willow (*Salix integra* 'Hakuro-Nishiki') at the lower end of the ellipse (pages 232–33). Here it could enjoy pride of place and lift the feeling of this area, which we designed to reflect the practical, down-to-earth nature of an abandoned barn foundation, a calf pen, and a milking parlor.

The Paddock

THE NORTHWEST CORNER of the property, directly behind the back gable end of the house, has remained a quiet space. When we arrived in 1983, a magnificent old elm was growing near the junction of the two dirt roads. The elm, with a 4-foot-diameter trunk, appeared healthy then, but within a year it succumbed to Dutch elm disease. The power company gingerly removed it, and we replaced it with *Ulmus* 'Regal', a hybrid elm that had been developed by the nearby Harrisville, New Hampshire, breeding program. We also planted hemlocks and balsam fir along the north

9.13 SUMMER *Three years ago, Dan Snow, dry stone waller and author of* In the Company of Stone, *built this new wall to look old. That's just what we wanted.*

206

edge of the area to screen us from the road. We then planted the golden-twigged dogwood as well as *Cornus stolonifera* 'Cardinal', for their bright winter colors against the dark evergreen trees, along with a yellowwood (*Cladrastis lutea*). But truth be told, we did little indeed with this back section of our garden; our attention was held in the main parts of the garden.

In the winter of 2002, we were looking north out our dining room window talking about what we would do with the area that coming spring. We discussed planting the whole area in shrubs, but we didn't want to block our view of the Ranneys' fields, which we could see down the length of the dirt road. We considered perennial borders, but we already had a high-maintenance garden. We talked about planting more specimen trees, but that would throw more shade onto the already shady north side of the house. Then Mary hit it.

Providing New Ideas

BECAUSE WE HAD CREATED so many complex areas in the garden, this last area along our itinerary should be as simple as possible (Y on map). Mary suggested we build a stone-wall-enclosed area that would read like a paddock (9.13). It was just the kind of use to which this area might have been put 200 years ago. We would replace the plantain-riddled "lawn" with proper sod once the wall was constructed. Outside the wall, particularly to the north, we would plant shrubs between the existing balsam firs and the back of the wall.

Our friend Dan Snow, a dry-stone waller, agreed to build the wall, but what kind of stone would we use? Dan could supply blocky mica schist, but such a refined wall would fly in the face of the nearby abandoned stone wall foundations. We wanted something rustic and even a bit rough to echo existing farmers' walls.

In the end we decided to use stone that would come from as close to our place as possible so the new stone would match old. Mary, who teaches in the two-room schoolhouse in the village, had been working with her colleague Claire Oglesby, who was retiring, selling her house, and moving to nearby Brattleboro. Knowing that I always need stone for clients, Claire mentioned to Mary that she

9.14 *(overleaf)* SUMMER *Our ewe and two lambs don't often get out of the paddock Dan Snow built for them. These topiary frames are based on sketches Henry Moore, the British sculptor, made of sheep.*

had a broken-down barn foundation on her property that she wanted to sell. We bought the stone, then asked Ellis Derrig's boys, using a front loader, backhoe, and dump truck, to transport the old wall the 6 miles to our place. They filled a 7-cubic-yard dump truck nine times, depositing the stone in piles along the length of the proposed wall.

As I was rousting around the old foundation during removal, Claire pointed out several 5- to 6-foot-wide thin, flat pieces of mica schist that had been piled up in her woods for as long as she could remember. She asked if I wanted to buy those as well; you know my answer. The Derrigs brought those over on the last load. Then, with their backhoe, we set them within the pea-stone sitting area between barn and pool as a base for chairs and planted pots (9.5).

In the fall and early winter of 2002, Dan Snow, one of a handful of American wallers certified by the British Dry Stone Wallers Association, began work on the wall. He brought along Ed Grady, a waller he had worked with at a workshop in Lexington, Kentucky, where Ed was from, and they built the 180 feet of wall (9.15). We designed three gaps in it; at some point we'll have rustic gates made out of split black locust, in keeping with the area's role as a paddock to enclose animals.

Create a Sense of Humor

MARY CAME UP with a marvelous idea for what to plant within the paddock. Nothing. We removed the old lawn and replaced it with Kentucky bluegrass sod, and that was it for plants. Mary felt we should add three garden ornaments. A paddock needs to enclose animals; we should have three topiary sheep. Through the Internet, we arranged with Jeff Brees, a California-based topiary frame maker, to create an alert-looking ewe and two lambs. We put them in the stone-wall-enclosed paddock and stuffed them with long-strand sphagnum moss (9.14); we'll build three gates to keep them in.

9.15 SUMMER
This final garden area along our itinerary takes us into the past and present: Mary's childhood among her family's sheep and the

*history of sheep in Vermont that
stretches up to today with our
neighbors Cindy and David
Major's prize-winning sheeps'
milk cheeses.*

10

The Garden *at* Courtyard House

I N 1995, TWELVE YEARS INTO WORK in our Vermont garden, we purchased a cottage in the village of Blockley, in the North Cotswold Hills of England. Courtyard House — houses are named in England (10.1) — is about 3 miles from Chipping Campden, near where Mary grew up; her mother was born in Blockley, her family's farm where her brother Simon lives and still works is only 5 miles away.

When we first stayed in the cottage in the spring of 1996, we looked down from the north-facing bedroom window onto the existing garden — an irregularly shaped outdoor space approximately 18 feet wide and 35 feet long. Its small, free-form central lawn was planted around the edges with a mix of shrubs (page 216: 1). A thriving *Viburnum tinus*, a 7-foot-high *Lonicera nitida* 'Baggesen's Gold', and a *Choisya ternata* screened us from our neighbor's garden, though two mockorange (*Philadelphus coronarius*) prevented us from seeing into our neighbor Margaret Stuart Turner's lovely back garden and the woodland beyond. There was an attractive purple-flowering *Hebe* in the heart of the garden along with many familiar varieties of perennials we grow here in Vermont: *Alchemilla mollis*, *Epimedium* x *rubrum*, the usual *Iris sibirica* hybrids, and peonies, among others.

10.1 SUMMER *We dine under the branches of this luminous chartreuse-leaved locust* (Robinia pseudoacacia *'Frisia'*).

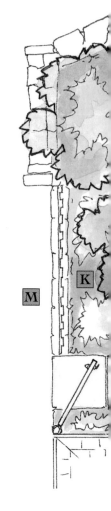

10.2 SUMMER *Wisteria intertwines among the letters of the name of our cottage.*

Perimeter Gardens Don't Engage

WE HAD INHERITED the classic perimeter garden—that is, plantings around the edge of a central lawn. It's a gardening style you might recognize because they are everywhere across North America. The problem with perimeter gardens is that they do not engage. We walk past plants, not among them, and therein lies a world of difference. In that first year, we walked out the sitting room doors, over the stone terrace, down onto the lawn, around the lawn's perimeter, and back into the house. Now that's a gardening nonevent. The only place to sit was on the quarter-circle stone patio, set into the ell of the house, where we felt remote from and literally one step above our garden. When we first visited Courtyard House with the real estate agent, a clothes drying rack sat in a sunny spot on the lawn. That said it all.

We wanted to be out there, sitting at a table in a garden having lunch with friends among fragrant, colorful plants; we wanted to be gardening among new perennials and shrubs and deciding where to put a well-chosen garden ornament. We couldn't live in this existing garden. We couldn't be in a garden divorced from the house, and we sure didn't need to haul in a lawn mower every week or so to mow a tiny lawn.

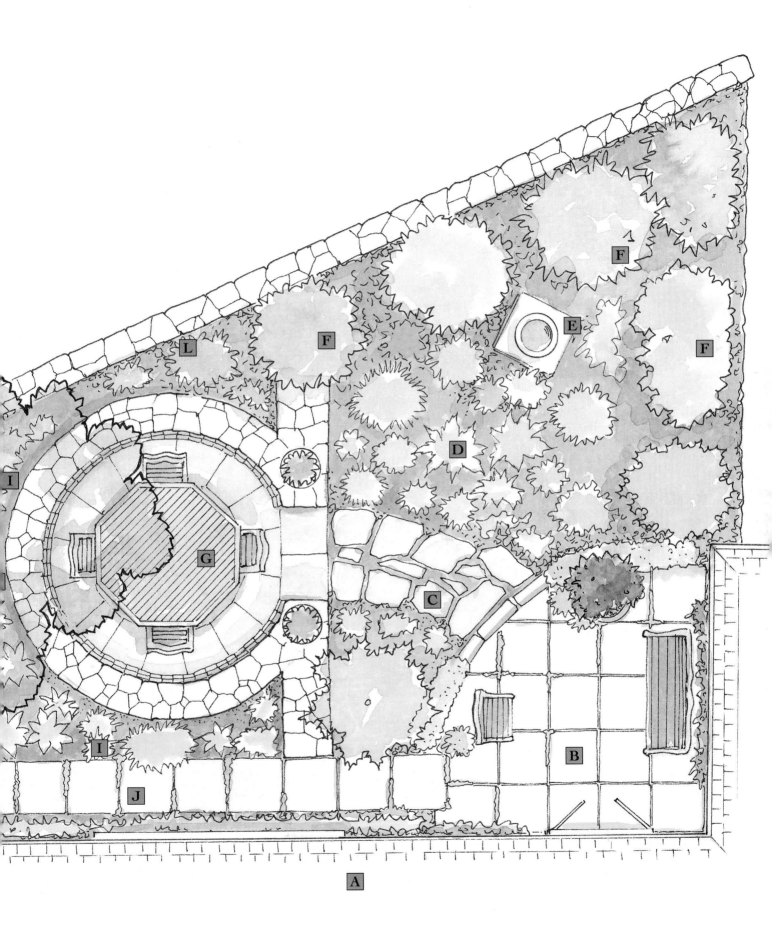

The Well-Chosen Tree

THERE WAS, HOWEVER, one literal bright spot: a ten-year-old *Robinia pseudoacacia* 'Frisia' planted on the west edge of the garden, near the stone wall that separated parking area from enclosed garden (10.1). Even on a rainy day during the growing season, its chartreuse-yellow leaves in our north-facing garden give the impression of sunlight.

We bought the cottage knowing we would initially be able to stay there only two weeks or so a year. The rest of the time we would rent it out by the week to people who wanted to visit the area and its many gardens open to the public. For six years, Chris

Installation: Before, During, and After

1. MARCH 1996 *We inherited the classic perimeter garden: central lawn with shrubs and perennials around the edges.* 2. FEBRUARY 1997 *Preparing to lay the circular dining area and connecting fieldstone path.* 3. JULY 2003 *We can now live in our garden.*

and Jane Gooding looked after the house and garden. Now Paul Williams, a garden designer, writer, and friend who lives nearby, oversees the garden with the help of Debbie Head.

Because our attention was first focused on renovating the interior of the cottage, we waited almost two years before redesigning the outside. In retrospect, that delay was fortuitous. We came to understand the 1,400-square-foot house and the fact that we wanted the garden to feel like an extension of it, thereby making the whole place feel roomier.

How Will You Live in Your Garden?

WE STARTED the design process by thinking through how we wanted to live outdoors: have meals outside at a table that sat at least four; have a place where eight to ten could gather; and surround these two sitting areas with plants and no lawn.

The fact that we had three distinct uses for the garden (sitting, dining, gardening) brings up a central element of small garden design. Creating two or even three centers of activity in a small garden makes it feel bigger than it really is, especially if all the areas are visible from windows looking out or down onto the garden. By creating more than one area of activity, we also break down the larger design problem into two or three parts, thereby easing the design process. We knew that the existing quarter-circle cut-stone patio would hold as many as eight chairs; that would be our main outdoor gathering space.

But where would we create a stone-paved area for a dining table and chairs? The sunny area right outside the French doors? Under the branches of the *Robinia*? Or somewhere in between the two? We considered putting a grape arbor under the *Robinia* and paving a dining area under it; the arbor would provide increased separation from the nearby parking area. We dropped that idea because a large structure would dominate a small space. We also considered putting the dining table in the sunniest, broadest part of the garden and surrounding it with perennials, thereby enabling us to develop the shade garden under the *Robinia*. That solution limited the amount of space for sun-loving perennials, and having the sky be the roof was not cozy. We decided to remove the two mockorange shrubs to open up a vista into our neighbor's back garden (page 216: 2), then set the dining area just under the easternmost branches of the *Robinia* so they would form a canopy over the table and chairs.

Light/Shade Variation

BECAUSE WE HAD LITTLE ROOM to take advantage of light variation, we made careful decisions. We had an area only roughly 15 feet by 15 feet in which we could plant sun-loving perennials; they would get direct sunlight from 9:00 A.M. until 3:00 P.M. during most of the growing season. When at the table, we

10.3 JULY 2003 *A view from the dining table.*

would be in full sun for breakfast, in filtered shade for lunch, and full shade for dinner.

I carefully pruned the *Robinia* of all its inner twigs and branches—those that got little direct sunlight—to allow as much sun as possible to filter onto the table and surrounding garden. I also removed all exterior branches above the dining table up to about 10 feet. But I allowed branches on the driveway side to arch down to provide privacy. Now we had to design the dining area.

Old Features Inspire New Ones

W HEN WE BOUGHT the cottage, a 10-foot-radius quarter-circle stone patio had already been built into the ell of the house (10.3) with a bench set on it; the patio was and remains connected to a York stone walkway through a stone wall and gate to the parking area. When it came time to design the dining area, we looked to the existing quarter-circle for inspiration. We used the theme of the circle and a part thereof for the new dining area to make new feel right with old. We designed a 10-foot-diameter stone-paved circle on which to set our dining table and chairs, then linked the old quarter-circle to the new full circle with an arcing fieldstone path that was also on a radius (10.6 and page 217). In this way the circle became the organizing form, fusing new to old through both material and shape.

Because we wanted to set the circle under at least some of the east branches of the *Robinia*, we had to create a flat surface on the slightly sloping ground under the tree. We designed a 12-inch-high omega-shaped retaining wall that would enable us to leave 75 percent of the soil under the *Robinia* undisturbed, thereby leaving its surface roots intact. The low wall would in turn define the perimeter of the circle for the dining table and chairs, though we would leave a gap in the wall to provide access to the dining area.

We then had to decide what kind of stone to use for the wall. New manufactured Cotswold wall stone, available in light-colored pressed aggregate blocks, would clash with the old. Again, existing features in the garden provided clues. We wanted stone that would match that in the existing walls, and we wanted to match the construction style of the old walls. Through mail and fax from Vermont to England, we found a source of old mossy wall stone at a nearby reclamation yard.

10.4 JULY *Put your thumb over the urn and watch this little garden lose its center, its focus.*

But what material to use for the circular dining area within that new low wall? Tightly fitted flat wall stones? Tamped crushed gravel? Again, we consulted existing features. Knowing that too many paving materials in a small garden can create incoherence, we repeated the look of the York stone that already made up the surface of the quarter-circle sitting area. We found a supplier of cast Cotswold stone circles for just such an application—a 9-foot-diameter circular dining surface. In a year or two it would weather to virtually the same color as the existing York stone, and cost about a third of what custom-cut York stone costs.

Having ordered and seen to the delivery of all the materials well ahead of time, we traveled to England in the spring of 1998 with Scott Wunderle and Scott Bolotin, two highly skilled members of my installation crew, to build the stone wall and paved circle within it. We installed the precast stone circle within the stone retaining wall, which looked wonderful from our bedroom window, then used some of the flat leftover wall pieces to create the short linking pathway between the quarter-circle patio and the new circular dining area. We then prepared the soil for planting, something we would do when we returned in August of that year.

But there was still a surprise in store for us that spring when we all sat down at the table for the first time. Mary realized, from her east-facing chair, that by pruning the height of the *Lonicera nitida* 'Baggesen's Gold' a couple of feet, we could see nearly half of the 500-year-old tower of Blockley Church (10.3). It was a marvelous serendipity, reminding us that chance is a partner in this act of conscious design.

What to Keep? What to Add?

UPON OUR RETURN in August, we had to decide what existing plants in the garden to leave and which to remove. We kept the *Choisya* for its year-round interest and beautiful shiny deep evergreen leaves and the purple-flowering *Hebe* because it was in just the right place at the edge of the existing patio. We also wanted to keep the *Lonicera nitida* 'Baggesen's Gold' because it screened us from our neighbor's garden and, with its yellowish leaves, echoed those of the *Robinia*. We removed other ailing shrubs as well as every perennial that we could grow in Vermont, but for some reason we kept a large *Epimedium* x *rubrum*.

The Gloucestershire County Council required us to discard all garden refuse by snipping every shrub, branch, and twig into pieces small enough to fit in 50-gallon green plastic recycling bags. The refuse would go into a special compartment in the rubbish trucks for transport to a recycling center. When we were finished clearing the garden of unwanted shrubs and perennials, we had a stack of at least twenty-five bags piled for pickup.

10.5 *(opposite)* JULY *The quarter circle of York stone in the ell of the house extends the living room space out into the garden; the bench echoes interior furniture, fusing outside to inside.*

10.6 *(overleaf)* JULY *We now live within our little garden rather than simply walking past it.*

With trees and shrubs now in leaf, we looked to the garden for clues to choosing plants within a theme. The dramatic chartreuse leaves of the *Robinia* gave us our first idea. We chose plants with either yellow flowers or foliage for both shade and sun to pull the *Robinia's* yellow color down to ground level. We chose other plants with flowers or foliage in a color range that looked good next to yellow: oranges, purples, blues, whites, burgundy reds, chartreuse, and dark green. Because this was a small garden, we also looked for perennials with long-lasting flowers and/or colorful foliage.

Now that we had chosen the broad variables that set the limits for plant choice, it was time to visit Bob Brown's Cotswold Garden Flowers Nursery, which had been getting a lot of attention in gardening circles both in the United Kingdom and the United States. A fine nursery can set your plant choices in a whole new direction.

The minute we saw the quality and variety of Bob Brown's plants, we knew what many of our plant choices would be. Off our wall would come the straggly rose we inherited; up would go (slowly) *Parthenocissus henryana*, which we had admired at the Campden House gardens. Out would go *Alchemilla mollis*; in would go *Saxifraga cortusifolia*. Out would go the *Centranthus ruber* that had insinuated itself into sections of the stone wall; in would go *Corydalis flexuosa* 'China Blue' and 'Nightshade' and a few *Pulmonaria saccharata* 'Mrs. Kittle' for the shady area.

We chose other plants for the yellow they introduced on the ground: *Hakonechloa macra* 'Aureola', with its yellow variegation (10.7); *Crocosmia solfaterre*, with its apricot-yellow flowers; *Sedum* 'Gold Mound'; *Digitalis lutea*; *Euonymus japonicus* 'Aureo-variegatus'; *Tiarella* 'Tigerstripe'; and a coppiced *Catalpa bignonioides* 'Aurea', to name a few.

Then we chose plants with flowers and/or foliage that would create pleasing contrasts with yellow foliage and yellow-flowering plants: *Heuchera* 'Plum Pudding', for its burgundy red foliage; *Saxifraga fortunei rubrifolia*, with its bronze foliage; *Acer palmatum* Dissectum 'Garnet'; and *Photinia x fraseri* 'Red Robin', for a terracotta pot just outside the sitting room doors (10.5), as well as a range of sun-loving ornamental grasses.

For contrast, we planted the tiny blue-flowering *Gentiana*

10.7 JULY *The urn is central to the garden and links the man-made world of the interior to the exterior.*

cachemirica next to the chartreuse *Thymus* 'Doone Valley' in the pathway. We also wanted large-leaved white-variegated plants, so we planted *Pulmonaria montana* 'David Ward' and *Brunnera macrophylla* 'Dawson's White'.

Then there were plants for unusual contrasting texture: *Stipa tenacissima*, with its long-lasting silky blonde foliage; *Euphorbia characias* x *robbiae*, with its green-yellow flowers; *Astrantia major* 'Claret', to provide deep red-yellow contrast; *Heuchera* 'Chocolate Ruffles', with its chocolate-burgundy foliage; and the gray foliaged *Eryngium bourgatii* 'GST Selected', for contrast. We left Bob Brown's with 118 plants. Our *Epimedium* x *rubrum* was doomed. We planted our new treasures in a white heat, paying some attention to a rough plan we had devised and a lot of attention to how the plants looked as we set them, still in pots, on the ground next to one another. We barely slept that night; we turned on the outside light and sat, first on the chairs on the quarter-circle, then on the chairs at the dining table. We had made another garden; we could hardly believe it.

Choosing and Siting Ornaments

BECAUSE NO GARDEN can succeed without strong visual centers that anchor areas, we often use man-made objects such as terra-cotta pots, ceramic urns, or sculpture. These unchanging, solid objects in an otherwise ever-changing garden add visual stability and stand in pleasing contrast to flowers and foliage. Once the garden was complete, we turned our attention to selecting and siting just the right number of ornaments to lift the tone of the garden, give it some variety, yet not create a busy look. First, we wanted to emphasize the feeling of enclosure on the quarter-circle sitting area, but we didn't want to block views into our tiny garden. We bought a finely made terra-cotta pot for the *Photinia* x *fraseri* 'Red Robin'. To gently emphasize the entrance to the stone-wall-enclosed dining area, we bought a matching pair of shallow basket-weave pots with handles from nearby Whichford Pottery to hold wild strawberry plants (*Fragaria vesca* 'Perpetual') (10.6).

To provide a strong center for the sunny perennial garden, and to help draw attention to that area when seen through the sitting room windows, we purchased a light-colored ceramic urn from nearby Batsford Arboretum Garden Centre and set it within the perennial garden, thereby providing a pleasing background for the dark red leaves of the annual *Phormium* (10.7).

Built and Living Screening

A S WE SAT in the garden and walked around in it, we realized that the stone wall behind which our red rental car was parked did not provide enough separation. We also knew we didn't want to add to that wall for fear of creating too dominating a structure. In the end, we designed a wooden trelliswork fence to run along the top of the wall, then arch up and over the existing gateway and attach to the house (10.8). The fence separated garden from parked cars, yet we could still see through the open trelliswork. The fence made the garden feel bigger by defining the space while creating a pleasing contrast between solid stone wall and open trelliswork. The lowest back branches of the *Robinia* now arc almost down to the top of the fence, creating a visual link between wall, fence, and tree.

A Leitmotif

W HILE DESIGNING the trellis, we looked closely at the existing metal gate (10.8). The gate maker included the quatrefoil at its four corners and center. We repeated this quatrefoil in the trellis atop the wall to visually tie fence to gate, thereby making this new object in the garden echo an existing feature. This leitmotif forms a shape we will at some point pick up again, thereby adding a subtle note of coherence within this small garden.

One lovely postscript to this little element in the garden helps link garden to church. After we pruned the *Lonicera* to expose more of the church tower across the street, we realized that stonemasons who built the church had repeated the quatrefoil many times on the church tower.

10.8 SUMMER *The gate, wall, and trellis separate the garden from the parking area while establishing all the feelings that gather around thresholds and entries.*

Around the Front Door

WHEN WE PURCHASED Courtyard House, we inherited two broad-leaved evergreens on either side of the front door: an *Aucuba japonica* 'Variegata', planted in a rapidly decomposing half-whiskey barrel; and a white-flowering camellia, struggling in a terra-cotta pot held together with wire. We replaced both containers and added a third—terra-cotta rather than ceramic, glazed, or cast stone, because terra-cotta went well with the honey-colored stone of our house and because this traditional material felt right for this nearly 300-year-old house. We purchased these new pots following the limits set by the concept of theme and variation: theme—terra-cotta; variation—color and size. We transplanted the

10.9 SUMMER *Concrete and driveway come right up to the foundation, so we have to rely on potted plants for our entry garden. How the wisteria grows in an 18-inch-wide planting strip between driveway and foundation is beyond me.*

Aucuba into a 24-inch-diameter terra-cotta pot and the camellia into a slightly smaller pot, then the dramatic ornamental grass *Stipa gigantea* underplanted with *X Heucherella* 'Kimono' in the third pot (10.9). The foliage of these plants would remain intact throughout the growing season.

Small Gardens Require Restraint

DESIGNING A SUCCESSFUL small garden requires restraint. We chose plants in light of the color of the *Robinia*; we limited ourselves to natural Cotswold stone for the retaining wall and the short arcing walkway. The circle and quarter-circle created a unified ground plan; we chose garden furniture made only of teak. By restraining ourselves regarding materials and layout, we created a structure in which a wide variety of plants could flourish within a coherent design, and a richly planted garden in which we could live.

Elements of Design for a Small Garden

- Create more than one center of activity to increase the feeling of size in the garden.
- Use screening to create a separation from other gardens, to divide the small space into two parts, or to tightly frame a distant view to co-opt it into your garden.
- Use paving materials to help define each area, but limit paving materials to one or two to ensure coherence; too many paving materials result in incoherence.
- Use simple paving patterns.
- Use garden ornaments or potted plants to mark entrances.
- Keep the forms and shapes simple, elegant, and geometric. Avoid fussy curves.
- Take advantage of your longest view.
- Look to your existing garden and its major plants or to your house and its colors for color scheme clues.
- Take advantage of shady and sunny areas.
- Consider where you will sit and how you will move within your small garden. Pave the areas most difficult to plant.
- Use paths to create unity and itinerary even in the smallest gardens.

APPENDIX A:
Maintaining Our Garden

MAINTAINING OUR GARDEN is striking a balance between the look of the garden and its health and design. In every job we do, whether raking leaves, weeding dandelions, or pruning a magnolia, we keep these goals in mind. When we edge a lawn path, for example, the garden looks much better; we've prevented grass from competing with perennials at the edge of a bed, thereby increasing their health; and we are maintaining a design balance implied by the visually strong edge between bed and lawn.

Maintenance Sets Tone
One result of the thirty to sixty hours of maintenance we put into our garden weekly is the tone and mood set by our work. We want the garden to feel relaxed and approachable. We don't want to create a tour de force of design or maintenance, because that would draw undue attention to itself rather than the garden as a whole. When a garden is maintained so that it is allowed to be, albeit within certain bounds, the tone, style, and feeling of being in the garden remain gently intact.

We once saw the opposite of what we're after. We walked into a mixed border and were struck not by the beauty of the garden but by the hundreds of bamboo stakes holding up dahlias, hollyhocks, and all manner of perennials and annuals. It was a tour de force of staking. This approach to garden maintenance drew attention to itself, thereby lifting that area out of the otherwise coherent broader garden. We certainly don't want our 7-foot-high blooms of *Crambe cordifolia* flopping onto their neighbors, so we do stake, but in such a way that the stems and leaves hide the stakes, thereby allowing the plant to be itself.

Design Guides Maintenance
The way we maintain our garden is harmonious with the overall effect we want to create. We live a rural life, so staking and tying up and edging to perfection would be inconsistent with the relaxed, easy feel the place calls for. That doesn't mean we're sloppy. Just watch Mary, with her high English standards, weed, and you'll know we are definitely not sloppy. The maintenance style we're after is appropriate for our garden. We want the beauty of the garden to slowly reveal itself, not overwhelm with our extraordinary design or maintenance skills.

Maintenance Is Management
This appendix organizes various elements of maintenance by the passage of the year, although it is by no means an exhaustive how-to. Rather we look at the principles that lie behind the work. Maintenance is about knowing the when and why of doing all the jobs that keep a garden in good heart and balance. We view maintenance as management. For example, we wait for the seeds of the *Phlox divaricata* in the Woodland Garden to ripen before string-trimming the spent flower heads. This timing means that the act of trimming also spreads seed that will regenerate the plants. On the other hand, we are quick to deadhead *Allium aflatunense* the moment the flowers begin to backslide. Managing *Allium aflatunense* this way prevents the setting and distribution of seed, so we don't have to weed out thousands of seedlings the following spring.

Maintenance is the larger, overall effort of managing the changes implied in growth, decline, and decay. Maintenance is much broader than weeding. Planting is creative; maintenance is sustaining and creative.

Having said this, maintenance is not romantic; it is hard, sometimes repetitive work. I was particularly aware of this when attending a one-day garden design symposium at Harvard University in the late 1980s, when America's interest in

gardening was cranking up. People had traveled from across the country to listen to world experts. When it came time for questions and answers, a woman from California asked, "What's it like not to be able to garden year-round here in New England?" A chorus of us gardeners from the Northeast chimed in unison, as if on cue, "It's wonderful!"

What's wonderful about it is the opportunity to stand back between mid-November and early April from all the hoeing, raking, edging, pruning, shearing, planting, uprooting, dividing, hauling, digging, and weeding to take a fresh look. Certainly winter is the time for pruning fruit trees, for removing dead or ailing trees and shrubs, for doing all the work that would otherwise endanger herbaceous perennials. It is also time for a cup of tea, a good read about gardening, and storing up energy for the burst, and I mean *burst* of activity once the snow has melted.

SPRING

■ TIDYING UP

We make a quick start in spring, working right up to the edge of the receding snow. We don't want matted leaves inhibiting the growth of daffodils, especially because their stems and buds often grow right through the snow. As the snow recedes, we pick up sticks and pluck leaves out of evergreen and deciduous woody plants. We cut back grasses and other perennials we left up for winter interest or because they don't like to be cut back in fall, as with *Perovskia atriplicifolia*, all the time being careful not to walk in the beds, where we would compact sodden earth. We deadhead daffodils after they bloom, rake all the lawns once the soil has dried out a bit, sweep stone paths and terraces, and place garden furniture and ornaments that have been stored in the barn all winter.

■ SPREADING COMPOST

Even though autumn is the better time to spread compost on the beds, spring works

best for us. Although we rake as many leaves as possible off the beds in fall, leaves invariably blow onto the garden until the first snowfall. So before spreading compost on the beds in spring, we rake them free of wet, matted leaves that have gathered here and there.

Then there was the autumn of 2002 when Mother Nature threw a mighty curveball. Even before all the leaves had fallen from the trees, a foot of snow fell in late October and again in early November. The following spring, the leaves on the beds were too wet and matted to be raked; we had to peel back sheets of them from hundreds of square yards of beds so the bulbs and perennials could grow and the earth could breathe. There was simply no time to spread compost that year.

■ TOOLS THAT WORK

We rely on certain tools that work for us:

- Dutch wheelbarrow, with its light plastic barrow
- Felco #2 pruning shears for Gordon; Felco #6 for Mary's smaller hands
- 5-gallon bucket to carry into the beds when weeding or collecting small sticks and debris
- Tarpaulin, a large surface spread on the ground on which to throw weeds, sticks, and debris, then drag to the burn or compost piles
- Hand hoe
- Rubber-palmed gloves with cloth backs for Mary
- Goatskin gloves made by Green Mountain Glove Company in Randolph, Vermont, from supple yet tough goatskin imported from Afghanistan—the finest work gloves I know
- Waterproof Muck Boots to keep our feet dry
- Hat to protect from overhead thorns, branches, and the sun

■ REPAIRING WINTER DAMAGE

Howard Andros once pointed out to me that gardening in Vermont is in some ways

easier than gardening on, say, the coast of Massachusetts. Snow cover is the key. When Vermont gets 10 inches of fluffy snow in November, large parts of coastal New England get rain. The rain freezes and damages the crowns of plants, whereas fluffy snow acts like a blanket throughout the winter. It keeps the ground at about 30 degrees Fahrenheit (unprotected soil might freeze 4 feet down) and protects the crowns of plants from subzero temperatures. (It's not uncommon for temperatures to drop to 25 degrees below zero in the dead of winter.)

But having that protective blanket of snow on the garden early each winter is not always the case. Winter sometimes causes a lot of damage here in Vermont. We often get snow before Thanksgiving; then in early December it rains. The snow melts, then nightly freezes, creating a crust of ice on the surface of the ground. One year in the early 1990s, 2 inches of ice formed followed by an icy crust of snow; those layers of ice remained throughout most of the winter. The crowns of herbaceous perennials were sealed off from the air by two layers of ice with snow between them. The crowns of so many plants suffocated that we had a shoebox full of plant labels the following spring from plants that had died. Ice also builds up on woody shrubs, weighing them down to the point where stems on brittle plants such as *Pieris japonica*, rhododendrons, and azaleas snap under the weight.

When gaps occur among shrubs or perennials in spring, we can do nothing else but look on the bright side—it's a chance to buy new plants.

■ MAKING AND MAINTAINING LAWN EDGES

After the soil has dried out a bit in early spring, we reestablish the dropped edges where lawn meets bed. We like these dropped edges because they allow us to bring sumptuous lawn paths right up to the edge of some beds yet define edges and draw clean lines between lawn and garden.

Edges, whether linear or broadly curving, clarify our intentions—this is lawn, that is garden—while also acting as a foil for the many shapes and forms of perennials and shrubs. Edges sharpen the image, and they are practical. Without dropped edges between garden and lawn, grass and clover would creep into the beds and before we knew it we would have the daunting task of taking up an entire garden to extricate grass roots from our perennials. Bed edges also ease lawn care, because I follow their lines on my riding mower.

I use a half-moon edger for cutting the turf to establish the edge. I then stand on the lawn and use a straight-nosed spade to cut the underside of the turf and lift the resulting sod into a wheelbarrow for composting or patching holes in the lawn.

Once established, lawn edges must be clipped every few weeks so they look sharp, not shaggy. Grass shears are the tool for this job; the half-moon edger is not. Shears are designed to cut blades of grass; the latter is meant to slice through turf. Because a half-moon edger removes a little bit of turf with every pass, over time the edge migrates farther and farther out from its original position, and weeds fill the space. To avoid that migration, use grass shears.

▪ CLEANING AND RENEWING GRAVEL PATHS

In spring, we rake the leaves and winter detritus from the 3/8-inch pea-stone paths, but invariably finely decomposed materials filter down into rather than stay atop the path. Over time this unsightly material builds up and makes the paths look dingy.

In 1992 when visiting Patrick Chassé, a Harvard-trained landscape architect who oversees the gardens of the late Abby Aldrich Rockefeller, I noticed that the surface of the gravel/pea-stone path had been raked into piles. Pat explained that every four or five years the maintenance crew rakes the surface material and simply wheelbarrows it out of the garden, then

wheelbarrows in new. It was clear that that is what must be done in order to keep pea-stone paths up to snuff. Ours have been in only about five years, and we haven't had to remove the top 2 inches yet, but this coming spring we may have to summon up the energy.

▪ DIVIDING AND TRANSPLANTING

We gardeners often find a reason not to take divisions of plants. It's hard work to divide a clump of ornamental grass. It's easier to say it looks so good during the winter from the study window that we should just let it grow, but the reality is, *Miscanthus oligostachys* 'Purpurascens' and all the other ornamental grasses have to be kept in their place through dividing or they'll take over America's gardens.

I have to put all of my 200 pounds on a stout shovel to get through the matted roots of maiden grass to secure a 1-foot-square division. And a single maiden grass can produce five plants in two or three gardening seasons. Then what do you do with them? We have just so many friends who are happy to take them. Once friends start saying no, we plant them in the nursery across the road, where they get so big in a couple of years that they take up more space than they deserve. I uproot them and put them not on the compost pile but the burn pile.

It's different with Siberian iris. They spread, but not with the nerve of ornamental grasses. We take divisions from the perimeter of the plant, then discard the stemless interiors. We take divisions of peonies following Alice Holway's rule: "The best time to transplant peonies is on October 15th, around noon." And we take divisions of daylilies practically whenever we want to. The problem with taking divisions is not the when and the why, it's finding the time, the energy, and the resolve to get down to it. It's much easier to say we'll do it in fall, we'll do it next spring, we'll do it when Robin and Siena are here, or when Pat can join us on a Saturday morning.

SUMMER

▪ COMPOSTING

A garden of one and a half acres produces a lot of compostable material, and we save every bit of it. When we weed and deadhead, when we empty the flower-pots every fall, when we rake clumps of grass left by the lawn mower in spring, when anything compostable comes out of the garden, we turn it into compost. And we use a simple method. We pile it across the road from the garden in 5- to 7-foot-high heaps, then every week or so I shovel previously made compost, with all the microbes in it, onto the top of the heap. We then just let it sit. If we have a hired backhoe in the garden, I always ask the operator to turn the piles; otherwise, we just let the material rot down. Once the compost is ready, we cover it with black plastic to keep weed seeds from getting into it.

▪ DEADHEADING

Herbaceous perennials are the most demanding, time-consuming plants in the garden. If you don't remove their spent blooms—that is, if you don't deadhead— perennials look awful. Many, such as the Shasta daisy *Leucanthemum x superbum* 'Becky', stop flowering, because too much energy goes into seed development. When we started our garden more than twenty years ago, we planted herbaceous perennials everywhere. Now that we have both reached the age of sixty, we are coming to terms with that decision. We no longer have the time or energy we had in our late forties. To reduce maintenance, we may well have to reduce the number of perennials and increase the number of woody flowering shrubs.

In the meantime, we do look after our perennials. When all the buds on a daylily stem have bloomed, for example, or the flowers of a hosta have gone by, the stem itself is still green. The temptation is to simply cut off the unsightly flower head near the top of the stem. The problem is that within a few weeks the stem browns off and spoils the plant's silhouette for the rest of the growing season. Instead, we reach well down within the foliage to cut off the spent flower stem as near to its base as possible. It is these little matters that have a huge impact on the garden's appearance.

Here are a few deadheading principles we keep in mind.

■ Regularly deadhead certain herbaceous perennials such as *Leucanthemum x superbum* 'Becky' and *Coreopsis verticillata* 'Moonbeam' to get more blooms.
■ Don't rush to deadhead plants that have attractive seed heads, such as peonies, *Allium christophii*, ornamental grasses, and *Fritillara bulgarica*.
■ Deadhead daily some perennials such as daylilies, whose spent blooms look bedraggled.

■ WEEDING

Weeding is one of those onerous tasks that can, in fact, become deeply engaging. But engagement relies on a feeling for detail and an abiding desire to care for and nurture plants.

I know full well that Mary is a far better weeder than I am. She has the patience and the sense of detail. While I'm off mowing half an acre of lawn, Mary is weeding, and when she is finished with a bed, it looks terrific. When I finish mowing the lawn, it looks terrific too.

There are certain things we do to prevent weeds from taking hold in the first place.

■ Use processed bark mulch under woody plants to inhibit weed germination.
■ Mass plants such as hardy geraniums (cranesbills) to shade the ground under crab apples, for example, thereby preventing sunlight from getting to the surface of the soil so weed seeds can't germinate.
■ Deadhead, to prevent the seeds of

aggressive plants that have gone to seed from dropping onto the soil.

Mary also has her weeding rules when weeds have taken hold.

- Remove weeds from the garden; don't simply hoe and leave the dead weeds on the surface.
- Weed all around plants, then lift the foliage to weed right up to the crown.
- Use your fingers when the weeds are small and in tight spaces.
- After weeding an area, till the surface to aerate it and scratch out any footprints.
- Kneel to weed as opposed to standing up and working with a hoe; it saves your back, and you can weed under plants more easily.
- Weed for a few hours every few days rather than many hours every other week. Don't let weeds get ahead of you.
- Attend to the details and be vigilant; weeding is as much about seeing as it is about work.

▪ HEDGE TRIMMING

I love trimming hedges. I think it has to do with the sense of order and pleasing contrast that trimmed hedges lend to natural plant forms. I use an electric hedge trimmer, and I always ask for help from Pat Sanzone, Robin Garlick, or Siena MacFarland, who have been helping us in the garden every Wednesday for the last couple of years.

While I'm setting up the 10-foot stepladder, whoever is helping me spreads plastic tarps along the drip line of the hedge. As I trim the hedge, the branch tips fall directly onto the tarp. In this way we cut out the whole cleanup stage of raking, making piles, and picking up the piles. I do the sides of the boxwood, yew, and viburnum hedges first, then the tops. I then turn to the teardrop-shaped *Acer campestre* trees at the top end of the Long Borders. Whereas Mary takes great satisfaction in weeding, I take equal satisfaction in hedge trimming.

FALL

▪ RAKING LEAVES

Indigenous and mature maples, black locusts, black cherries, and ash trees ring the garden. They all have leaves. Apple trees, Japanese tree lilacs, birches, stewartias, the cork tree, crab apples, lilacs, viburnums, and hydrangeas are all lovely, and they all have leaves. Then there are the hundred or so mature native trees along the hedgerow on the west side of the dirt road near our house. They all have leaves too. And every mid-October, these leaves fall to the garden. Those along the west hedgerow that don't actually fall on the garden are blown into it by the predominant west wind. I can tell you that it is one major project to gather these leaves and compost them, but that's what we've been doing for twenty years.

We can't leave the leaves on the garden. They get wet, mat down, and destroy the crowns of herbaceous perennials. So we rake and rake and rake, and we pile them all downwind of the garden so they don't blow back again. Over the years we have created mountains of leaf mold, a lot of which is stored and ready to go back onto the gardens each spring.

We gather these leaves by raking them onto 10-foot by 12-foot tarps, which we drag to the dump sites. I also use a mulcher attachment on my riding lawn mower. The minute leaves start to fall, I start to gather or mulch.

▪ PUTTING THE GARDEN TO BED

The fall is a bittersweet time of year in our Vermont garden. The orange, red, and yellow leaves look beautiful on the trees, especially against the deep blue autumn sky. They also look beautiful on the green lawn. But they have to be raked at the same time many other jobs must be accomplished:

- Bring in all the furniture and garden ornaments and store them in the barn;

freeze/thaw cycles can damage terracotta, cast stone, and teak.
- Cut back and compost all the herbaceous perennials, which, unlike ornamental grasses, won't look good in the garden through the winter.
- Burn the brush and pruning piles.
- Remove trees and shrubs that are ailing or have grown out of scale and create too much shade.
- Save perennials that dry well, such as hydrangea blooms, ornamental grasses, and *Sedum* (now *Hylotelephium*) *spectabile* flower heads, for dried winter bouquets.
- Dismantle the pots planted with annuals, and compost the soilless mix and the plants themselves.

▪ PLANTING TULIPS IN POTS

Because mice and voles can destroy tulips planted directly in the ground, we plant about twenty types of tulips in pots and keep them in the unheated part of the cellar. We fill perhaps thirty large pots with Pro-Mix, plant the bulbs, and water the pots well initially, then only monthly throughout the winter. In late March or early April, when shoots begin to appear, we haul the pots out of the cellar and set them in the garden, where they bloom remarkably well for at least three weeks or more.

After they complete their bloom, we transplant the bulbs into the garden across the road with their foliage intact and in subsequent years use them for cut flowers. Over time, mice and voles cause the planted tulips to decline, but we just keep planting replacements, which have kept us in cut tulips in early spring for years.

WINTER

▪ PRUNING

Pruning is sculpting. Although I prune crab apple and standard apple trees for flowers and fruit, although I prune stewartias and cork trees, lilacs, and viburnums for flowers, I am aware of how I am creating shapes and forms. As I prune the interior of crab apples and the big standard apple, I am aware of the lines and forms of the branches; I pay attention to how removing interior shaded branches helps show the interplay of trunk, branch, and twig. With my Felco #2s and pruning saw, I judiciously subtract, thereby creating cleaner forms in space.

ORGANIC MULCHES

We use organic mulches, which derive from plants, because they retain moisture in the soil while helping to control weeds, erosion, and muddy backsplash onto leaves, flowers, fruits, or vegetables. Mulches maintain an even soil temperature winter and summer, thereby encouraging beneficial microorganisms and bacteria while reducing the stress of temperature fluctuation on plants. As mulch decays over time and earthworms incorporate it into the soil, organic matter is added to the soil, thereby building up what is called tilth, or soil structure, which is especially important in organically starved gravelly, sandy, or clayey soils. Finally, mulches make our garden look good by providing a uniform and unifying color on the ground.

Whenever possible, we use mulches from our area: shredded bark mulch, white pine needles, shredded leaves from our trees and shrubs. After all, when we mulch, we are simply following nature's cue; if we didn't rake leaves or cut back perennials in the autumn, we would see that woody as well as herbaceous plants mulch themselves with their own leaves.

TIME OF APPLICATION

We apply mulch to existing gardens in late spring, after the soil has warmed up, and dried out a bit from heavy rains and melting snow. Mulch too early and we trap too much moisture in soil that therefore stays cold and sodden. We apply mulch to new perennials, shrubs, trees, and vegetables immediately after planting.

We apply about 2 inches of mulch around newly planted plants. Use less and the mulch will neither hold moisture nor

prevent weeds; use more and we run the risk of creating waterlogged soil and preventing oxygen from reaching surface roots. One exception to the rule is to mulch more heavily when planting in fall, then pulling all but 2 inches of that mulch away in spring. We keep mulch 3 to 6 inches from the trunks of trees, the stems of shrubs, and the base of perennials, vegetables, and annuals to promote air circulation and prevent rot.

MAINTENANCE

Once mulch begins to decompose late in the first or in the second year, weeds begin to appear on its surface. Because organic mulches are generally loose, weeds are easily pulled from it. There is no need to fork decomposed mulch into the beds; earthworms do that.

PROCESSED BARK MULCH

Because there is a firewood production mill within 15 miles of us that produces vast quantities of inexpensive finely ground bark mulch, we use a lot of it. We spread bark mulch 2 inches thick under shrubs and in a 2- to 3-foot-radius around established trees in the lawn. We also use it to form paths through the Woodland Garden, where it feels appropriate. We replenish this mulch every year; when it decomposes sufficiently, we spread the compost into adjacent beds and start all over again with a fresh layer.

SAWDUST

Sawdust is a long-lasting compost that we have found to be suitable under blueberries, raspberries, and gooseberries. Once dry, it forms a weed-defeating crust, but, unlike peat moss, the crust remains porous. As with all wood-based mulches, sawdust has a high carbon content. The microorganisms that break down wood require nitrogen, which will come from the soil in which plants grow. However, by simply spreading wood-based mulches on the surface, they won't draw significant amounts of nitrogen away from the plants.

SHREDDED LEAVES

Because whole leaves form a dense, wet mat over the winter, we don't use them for mulch in perennial borders, where they can cause plant crowns to rot. We pile leaves downwind of the garden and allow them to compost themselves over a year's time. The result is a lovely leaf mold that plants thrive on. We spread it 3 to 4 inches thick on the soil around perennials in spring.

PINE NEEDLES

Howard Andros once showed me how he mulched recently planted or transplanted perennials with 2 to 3 inches of pine needles. They helped conserve moisture, and air could circulate among the loosely piled needles. He removed the needles after a few months, before they had time to decompose and acidify the soil. Pine needles are also the perfect mulch for acid-loving broad-leaved and needled evergreens. Though we have not gone to the effort of laying down pine boughs in late fall, many gardeners in our area use them as a winter mulch for perennial beds. They lay them onto beds after the top 2 inches of soil is frozen and leave them on until early spring.

STRAW AND HAY

Baled straw contains the dried, nearly grainless stems of barley, oats, or wheat, whereas hay contains the dried seeds of grasses and often weeds that grow in hayfields. Straw is weed free, whereas hay and weed seeds are throughout baled hay. Because straw has a stouter stem than that of hay, it stacks much like jackstraws; therefore, air and water can pass through it easily. We use straw under tomatoes, strawberries, and many vegetables that develop near the surface of the soil and would be damaged by soil splashing onto fruits during rain or irrigation. Straw or hay are good for mulching paths between rows of other vegetables as well as the soil under the vegetables themselves.

■ LAWN CLIPPINGS

Lawn clippings are rich in nitrogen, so they are best left on the lawn to decompose and rebuild the soil. However, during the spring or other wet periods when the lawn grows 3 inches in three days, clippings build up on our lawn. We rake up the clumps of cut grass immediately after mowing and compost it or put it under the raspberries, being careful not to lay down more than 3 to 4 inches; lay down more than that and within two to three hours fermentation will start and the clippings will sour. A thin layer of nitrogen-rich lawn clippings is excellent as a mulch for vegetables as well as flowering annuals, but never under perennials. Because we don't use any chemicals on our lawn, or anywhere else in the garden, we use the clippings without being concerned that chemicals will find their way into our fruits and vegetables.

■ COCOA-BEAN AND BUCKWHEAT HULLS

We tried mulching with cocoa bean and buckwheat hulls several years ago but found them both unsatisfactory in this area of the country, which gets 44 inches of rain a year. After a rain, cocoa bean hulls mat together. If they stay wet for even two or three days, an unsightly white mold forms atop the mats. And when dry, the hulls are easily blown about. Buckwheat hulls are preferable, but we have stopped using both. Given the cost and the fact that they last only one season, we found that the most appropriate use for these mulches is 2 inches in small rose, herb, or perennial beds, or just to cover the soil in pots planted with annuals.

■ WOVEN LANDSCAPE FABRIC

We have found that woven black plastic landscape fabric creates more problems than it solves in the ornamental garden. It prevents perennials from spreading, and weeds grow in the decomposing mulch atop the fabric. Their roots go through the gaps in the weave and take hold in the soil below. What usually results is a mess. We have, however, successfully used it under newly planted shrubs. We cover the fabric with 2 inches of processed bark mulch, which we renew annually; it helps control weeds under woody plants. Of course, its use precludes planting ground covers. Having said all this, there is something unsatisfying about using any form of plastic in the garden.

Peony 'Claudia',
Siberian iris, hardy
geraniums, hollyhocks,
yews, and a pollarded
silver willow—it all
sounds like an English
cottage garden to me
except for the black
locust logs, upright.

APPENDIX B:
Plants in the Vermont Garden

COMMON NAMES VARY across North America; those I show in these appendices derive from *Hortus Third*, though common names in your area may vary. Given the ever-changing nature of taxonomy and nomenclature, I have done my best to record the most up-to-date binomials for the plants listed here.

South Side of House and Barn, Including Entry Garden

■ WOODY PLANTS

Acer palmatum 'Twombly's Red Sentinel' (bloodgood maple)
Betula platyphylla japonica (Japanese whitespire birch)
Corylus avellana 'Contorta' (Harry Lauder's walking stick)
Juniperus conferta (shore juniper)
Larix decidua 'Pendula' (weeping larch)
Paxistima canbyi (cliff green, mountain lover)
Physocarpus opulifolius Diabolo™ (purple-leaved ninebark)
Pinus sylvestris 'Nana' (dwarf Scots pine)
Rhamnus frangula 'Asplenifolia' (alder buckthorn)
Taxus x media 'Hicksii' (Hicks yew)
Viburnum lantana 'Mohican' (wayfaring tree)

■ HERBACEOUS PERENNIALS

Amsonia hubrechtii (bluestar)
Aquilegia canadensis (American columbine)
Aster nova-angliae, in variety (New England asters)
Cerastium tomentosum (snow-in-summer)
Euphorbia amygdaloides 'Purpurea' (spurge)
Euphorbia dulcis 'Chameleon' (purple-leaved spurge)
Geranium x oxonianum 'Claridge Druce' (cranesbill)
Helictotrichon sempervirens 'Sapphire' (blue oat grass)

Hemerocallis 'Cherry Cheeks' (daylily)
Hylotelephium spectabile 'Brilliant'
Leymus secalinus (blue lyme grass)
Miscanthus sinensis 'Strictus' (porcupine grass)
Miscanthus sinensis 'Yakushima' (maiden grass)
Nepeta x faassenii 'Blue Wonder' (catmint)
Panicum virgatum 'Shenandoah'
Phalaris arundinacea (canary reed grass)
Sedum 'Mohrchen' (stonecrop)
Sedum acre
Sedum spurium 'Ruby Mantle'
Sempervivum spp.
Stachys byzantina 'Silver Carpet' (lamb's ears)

■ BULBS

Allium aflatunense (flowering onion)
Crocuses, in variety
Daffodils, in variety
Galanthus nivalis 'Flore Pleno' (snowdrops)
Leucojum aestivum 'Gravetye' (snowflakes)

Crab Apple Allées

■ TREES

Malus 'Adams'
Malus 'Prairiefire'
Malus Sugar Tyme®

■ HERBACEOUS PERENNIALS

Geranium x oxonianum 'Claridge Druce'
Geranium platypetalum
Geranium praetense 'Brookside'

West Shrub Border

■ WOODY PLANTS

Acer pseudosieboldianum (Korean maple)
Daphne mezereum (February daphne)
Euonymus fortunei
Fothergilla gardenii (witch alder)
Hydrangea paniculata
Hydrangea paniculata 'Tardiva'
Physocarpus opulifolius 'Dart's Gold' (yellow-leaved ninebark)
Syringa reticulata (Japanese tree lilac)
Syringa villosa (late lilac)

Daffodils and Fritillaria meleagris

Syringa vulgaris, whites and purples
Syringa vulgaris 'Sensation' (lilac)

■ HERBACEOUS PERENNIALS

Adiantum pedatum (maidenhair fern)
Ajuga reptans 'Caitlin's Giant'
Arisaema triphyllum (jack-in-the-pulpit)
Hosta 'Shade Fanfare'
Phlox stolonifera 'Blue Ridge' (creeping phlox)
Phlox stolonifera 'Bruce's White'
Phlox stolonifera 'Sherwood Purple'
Polystichum acrostichoides (Christmas fern)
Pulmonaria 'Roy Davidson' (lungwort)
Trillium viride

■ BULBS

Daffodils, in variety

Brick Walk Garden

■ WOODY PLANTS

Akebia quinata (five-leaved akebia)
Artemisia abrotanum (southernwood)
Azaleas, in variety
Berberis thunbergii 'Aurea' (yellow-leaved barberry)

A daylily and the annual Salvia *'Indigo Spires'.*

Berberis thunbergii 'Kobold' (Kobold
barberry)
Clematis recta (erect clematis)
Cornus alba 'Elegantissima' (variegated
Tartarian dogwood)
Euonymus fortunei 'Gaiety' (variegated
euonymus)
Fothergilla gardenii (witch alder)
Hedera helix 'Aurea' (yellow-leaved ivy)
Humulus lupulus 'Aureus' (yellow-leaved
hop vine)
Hydrangea paniculata
Hypericum kalmianum (St. Johnswort)
Lonicera x brownii (honeysuckle)
Lonicera x heckrottii (Heckrotti honeysuckle)
Lonicera prolifera (moonvine honeysuckle)
Lonicera x tellmanniana (Tellman's honey-
suckle)
Pinus strobus 'Nana' (dwarf white pine)
Pinus sylvestris 'Nana' (dwarf Scots pine)
Potentilla fruticosa 'Abbotswood' and
'Gold Drop'
Prunus x cistena (purple-leaved sand cherry)
Pyrus (seckel pear)
Rhododendron 'Pink and Sweet' (azalea)
Robinia pseudoacacia 'Frisia' (yellow-leaved
black locust)

Rosa glauca
Rubus cockburnianus 'Golden Vale' (bramble)
Salix alba (white willow)
Spiraea japonica 'Anthony Waterer' (Anthony
Waterer spirea)
Taxus x media 'Hicksii' (Hicks yew)
Thuja occidentalis 'Smaragd' (emerald
green arborvitae)
Wisteria 'Aunt Dee'
Wisteria sinensis 'Alba'

■ HERBACEOUS PERENNIALS

Achillea 'Coronation Gold' (yarrow)
Aconitum napellus (monkshood)
Actaea simplex 'Atropurpurea'
(purple-leaved snakeroot)
Alcea rosea (hollyhock)
Alchemilla mollis (lady's mantle)
Amsonia tabernaemontana (bluestar)
Angelica atropurpurea (giant angelica)
Angelica gigas (angelica)
Aruncus dioicus (goatsbeard)
Asarum canadense (American ginger)
Astilbe japonica 'Red Sentinel'
Baptisia australis (false indigo)
Bearded iris, in variety
Chenopodium bonus-henricus (good
King Henry)
Dicentra formosa 'Zestful' (everlasting
bleeding-heart)
Echinacea 'Bravado' (coneflower)
Eryngium alpinum 'Donard Variety' (sea
holly)
Euphorbia dulcis 'Chameleon' (purple-
leaved spurge)
Euphorbia polychroma (cushion spurge)
Festuca glauca 'Elijah Blue' (blue fescue)
Geranium macrorrhizum 'Spessart' (bigroot
geranium)
Geranium praetense 'Brookside' (cranesbill)
Geranium sanguineum lancastriense
(cranesbill)
Helenium 'Moerheim Beauty' (sneezeweed)
Hemerocallis 'Stella de Oro' (daylily)
Heuchera 'Chocolate Ruffles' (coralbells)
Heuchera 'Pewter Veil'
Heuchera micrantha 'Palace Purple'
Hosta 'Mediovariegata'
Hosta 'On Stage'
Hosta 'Sagae'

Hylotelephium 'Autumn Joy'
Hypericum frondosum
Iris sibirica, in variety (Siberian iris)
Leucanthemum x superbum 'Becky'
(Shasta daisy)
Miscanthus oligostachys 'Purpurascens'
(purple reed grass)
Nepeta 'Six Hills Giant' (catmint)
Paeonia 'Claudia' (peony)
Panicum virgatum 'Cloud Nine' (switch
grass)
Panicum virgatum 'Heavy Metal'
Papaver orientale (Oriental poppy)
Penstemon digitalis 'Husker's Red' (beard-
tongue)
Salvia x sylvestris 'Blue Queen'
Sanguisorba canadensis (burnet)
Sedum acre (stonecrop)
Sedum spurium 'Dr. John Creech'
Stachys byzantina, in variety (lamb's ears)

■ BULBS

Oriental lilies, in variety

*Switch grass (*Panicum virgatum *'Cloud
Nine') and balloonflower (*Platycodon
grandiflorus *'Fuji Blue').*

*Purple parsnip (*Angelica gigas*).*

Woodland Garden

■ WOODY PLANTS

Acer saccharum (sugar maple)
Corylus avellana 'Contorta' (Harry Lauder's walking stick)
Euonymus fortunei
Hamamelis x intermedia 'Diane' (witch hazel)
Hydrangea paniculata
Hydrangea paniculata 'Unique'
Lonicera x heckrottii (Heckrotti honeysuckle)
Magnolia stellata (star magnolia)
Prunus serotina (black cherry)
Pyrus ussuriensis (Chinese pear)
Rhododendron 'Aglo'
Robinia pseudoacacia (black locust, part of indigenous woods)
Stephanandra incisa 'Crispa'
Stewartia pseudocamelia
Viburnum dentatum (arrowwood)
Viburnum lantana 'Mohican' (wayfaring tree)
Virburnum rhydidophyllum
Vinca minor 'Bowles' and 'Purpurea' (periwinkle)

■ HERBACEOUS PERENNIALS

Adiantum pedatum (maidenhair fern)
Ajuga reptans 'Burgundy Glow' (bugleweed)
Ajuga reptans 'Gaiety'
Astilbes, in variety
Euphorbia polychroma (cushion spurge)
Hosta 'Albomarginata'
Hosta 'Blue Cadet'
Hosta 'Krossa Regal'
Hosta 'Mediovariegata'
Hosta 'Royal Standard'
Hosta 'Sum and Substance'
Hosta 'Sun Power'
Hosta sieboldiana 'Elegans'
Lamprocapnos spectabilis 'Alba' (white bleeding-heart)
Myrrhis odorata (sweet cicely)
Packera aurea (golden groundsel)
Phlox divaricata (blue woodland phlox)
Phlox divaricata 'Dirgo Ice' (woodland phlox)
Phlox stolonifera 'Blue Ridge', 'Bruce's White', 'Home Fires' 'Sherwood Purple' (creeping phlox)
Sanguinaria canadensis 'Flore Pleno' (double bloodroot)
Sasa veitchii (Kuma bamboo grass)
Tiarella 'Slick Rock' (foamflower)
Waldsteinia ternata (Siberian barren strawberry)

■ BULBS

Fritillaria meleagris (fritillary)
Hyacinthoides non-scripta (English bluebell)

Long Borders

■ WOODY PLANTS

Acer campestre (English hedge maple)
Betula platyphylla japonica (Japanese whitespire birch)
Buxus microphylla 'Green Mountain' (boxwood)
Buxus microphylla koreana (Korean boxwood)
Buxus sempervirens 'Variegata' (yellow-variegated boxwood)
Chamaecyparis pisifera 'Filifera' (thread cypress)
Clematis 'Henryi'
Fagus sylvatica 'Purpurea' (purple-leaved European beech)

Fraxinus pennsylvanica (northern ash)
Picea pungens 'Fastigiata' (fastigiate blue spruce)
Picea sitchensis 'Speciosa' (Sitka spruce), on a standard
Ruta graveolens (common rue)
Salix alba (white willow), pollarded
Sambucus nigra 'Madonna' (variegated elderberry)
Viburnum carlesii (mayflower viburnum)
Vinca minor (periwinkle)
Wisteria 'Aunt Dee'

■ HERBACEOUS PERENNIALS

Aconitum carmichaelii 'Arendsii' (monkshood)
Actaea simplex 'Atropurpurea' (purple-leaved snakeroot)
Alcea rosea (hollyhock)
Alchemilla mollis (lady's mantle)
Astrantia major 'Rosea' (masterwort)
Baptisia australis (false indigo)
Bearded iris, in variety
Calamagrostis acutiflora 'Karl Foerster' (feather reed grass)

*Switch grass (*Panicum virgatum *'Heavy Metal') and sneezeweed (*Helenium autumnale *'Riverton Beauty').*

Campanula latifolia (bellflower)
Cephalaria gigantea (giant scabious)
Crambe cordifolia
Daylilies, in variety throughout
Dianthus (pinks)
Dictamnus albus (gas plant)
Dipsacus fullonum (teasel)
Eupatorium maculatum 'Gateway' (Joe Pye weed)
Euphorbia dulcis 'Chameleon' (purple-leaved spurge)
Geranium macrorrhizum 'Spessart' (bigroot geranium)
Geranium phaeum 'Samobor' (mourning widow)
Geranium praetense 'Brookside' (cranesbill)
Gypsophila repens 'Rosea' (baby's breath)
Helenium 'Moerheim Beauty' (sneezeweed)
Heuchera (coralbell)
Heuchera 'Garnet' (coralbell)
Heuchera 'Palace Purple' (coralbell)
Heuchera americana (coralbell)
Hosta 'Sum and Substance'
Hylotelephium 'Autumn Joy'
Hylotelephium 'Vera Jameson'
Hylotelephium sieboldii 'Variegatum' (October plant)

*A hosta and maidenhair fern (*Adiantum pedatum*).*

Miscanthus sinensis 'Gracillimus' (maiden grass)
Miscanthus sinensis 'Morning Light' (morning light reed grass)
Miscanthus sinensis 'Purpurascens' (purple reed grass)
Miscanthus sinensis 'Variegatus' (variegated reed grass)
Paeonia 'Early Windflower'
Paeonia 'Roselette' (herbaceous peony)
Panicum virgatum 'Cloud Nine' (switch grass)
Pennisetum alopecuroides 'Hameln' (fountain grass)
Penstemon digitalis 'Husker Red' (beard-tongue)
Phalaris arundinacea (reed canary grass)
Salvia verticillata 'Purple Rain'
Stachys byzantina (lamb's ears)
Stachys macrantha 'Superba' (betony)

■ BULBS

Allium aflatunense (flowering onion)
Allium bulgaricum (syn. Nectaroscordum siculum bulgaricum) (Bulgarian allium)
Allium christophii (star of Persia)

Dining Area/Rock Garden/Wet Garden

■ WOODY PLANTS

Abies koreana 'Prostrate Beauty' (Korean fir)
Acer pseudosieboldianum (Korean maple)
Acer saccharum (sugar maple)
Buxus microphylla 'Green Mountain' (boxwood)
Buxus microphylla koreana (Korean boxwood)
Calluna, in variety (heather)
Clethra alnifolia (sweet pepperbush)
Cornus 'Midwinter Fire' (winter flame red-twigged dogwood)
Cornus alternifolia (pagoda dogwood)
Euonymus fortunei
Euonymus fortunei 'Emerald Gaiety' (variegated euonymus)
Fothergilla gardenii (witch alder)
Hydrangea petiolaris (climbing hydrangea)

*Purple reed grass (*Miscanthus sinensis 'Purpurascens'*), red-leaved barberry (*Berberis thunbergii 'Atropurpurea'*) —now removed from the garden.*

Juniperus procumbens 'Nana' (Japanese garden juniper)
Kerria japonica 'Variegata' (Japanese rose)
Magnolia stellata (star magnolia)
Microbiota decussata (Russian cypress)
Paxistima canbyi (cliff green, mountain lover)
Pinus mugo (mugho pine)
Pinus sylvestris 'Nana' (dwarf Scots pine)
Prunus serotina (black cherry)
Rhododendron 'Molly Fordham'
Spiraea japonica 'Alpina' (Japanese spirea)
Taxus baccata 'Repandens' (spreading yew)
Taxus canadensis (species yew)
Taxus x media 'Hicksii' (Hicks yew)
Tsuga canadensis 'Jeddeloh' (Jeddeloh dwarf hemlock)
Viburnum lantana 'Mohican' (wayfaring tree)
Viburnum opulus 'Nanum' (dwarf cranberry bush)

■ HERBACEOUS PERENNIALS

Alchemilla mollis (lady's mantle)
Anemone tomentosa 'Robustissima' (grape-leaved anemone)
Aruncus dioicus 'Kneiffii' (goatsbeard)

Astrantia major (masterwort)
Astrantia major 'Ruby Cloud'
Athyrium niponicum 'Pictum' (Japanese
    painted fern)
Belamcanda chinensis (leopard flower)
Brunnera macrophylla
Campanula 'Elizabeth'
Chelone lyonii (pink turtlehead)
Convallaria majalis (lily-of-the-valley)
Convallaria majalis 'Variegata' (variegated
    lily-of-the-valley)
Coreopsis verticillata (tickseed)
Geranium 'Ann Folkard' (cranesbill)
Geranium praetense 'Brookside'
Geranium psilostemon
Hemerocallis lilioasphodelus (lemon lily)
Heuchera 'Chocolate Ruffles' (coralbell)
Heuchera 'Petite Pearl Fairy'
Heuchera x heucherella 'Silver Streak'
Heuchera micrantha 'Palace Purple'
Hosta 'Aureomarginata'
Hosta 'Blue Cadet'
Hosta 'Krossa Regal'
Hosta 'Stiletto'
Hosta 'Sum and Substance'

*Tufted hairgrass (*Deschampsia
caespitosa*) and bigroot geranium
(*Geranium macrorrhizum *'Ingwersen's
Variety').*

Hosta sieboldiana 'Elegans'
Hylotelephium sieboldii 'Variegatum'
    (October plant)
Iris sibirica, in variety (Siberian iris)
Kirengeshoma palmata (yellow waxbells)
Lamium galeobdolon 'Herman's Pride'
    (variegated yellow archangel)
Lamium maculatum 'White Nancy' (dead nettle)
Ligularia stenocephala 'The Rocket'
    (ligularia)
Lobelia cardinalis (cardinal flower)
Lobelia siphilitica (blue lobelia)
Lysimachia nummularia 'Aurea'
    (yellow-leaved creeping Jenny)
Malva moschata (musk mallow)
Papaver orientale (Oriental poppy)
Podophyllum peltatum (mayapple)
Polemonium caeruleum 'Brise d'Anjou'
    (Jacob's ladder)
Pulmonaria 'Majesty' (lungwort)
Pulmonaria 'Roy Davidson'
Salvia verticillata 'Purple Rain' (purple
    rain sage)
Symphytum grandiflorum (comfrey)
Tiarella cordifolia 'Slick Rock' (foamflower)
Viola labradorica (Labradore violet)

Herb Garden

■ WOODY PLANTS

Actinidia kolomikta (kiwi vine)
Buxus microphylla koreana (Korean boxwood)
Caragana arborescens 'Pendula' (weeping
    pea shrub)
Clematis 'Nelly Moser'
Clematis paniculata
Cornus alternifolia (pagoda dogwood)
Fothergilla gardenii (witch alder)
Hydrangea petiolaris (climbing hydrangea)
Iberis sempervirens (candytuft)
Lavandula angustifolia 'Hidcote' (lavender)
Malus 'Royalty' (crab apple)
Rosa 'Mary Queen of Scots'
Rosa 'William Baffin'
Salix alba sericea (white willow)
Taxus x media 'Hicksii' (Hicks yew)
Teucrium chamaedrys (germander)
Thuja occidentalis 'Smaragd' (emerald
    green arborvitae)

*Katsura tree (*Cercidiphyllum japonicum*).*

Viburnum prunifolium (black haw,
    nannyberry)
Vitis 'Van Buren' (grape vine)

■ HERBACEOUS PERENNIALS

Actaea simplex 'Atropurpurea' (purple-
    leaved snakeroot)
Adiantum pedatum (maidenhair fern)
Alchemilla mollis (lady's mantle)
Allium schoenoprasum (chives)
Allium senescens glaucum
Armoracia rusticana 'Variegata' (variegated
    horseradish)
Dennstaedtia punctilobua (hay-scented fern)
Dianthus 'Ian' (pinks)
Dicentra formosa 'Aurora' (everlasting bleed-
    ing-heart)
Dicentra formosa 'Zestful'
Euphorbia polychroma (cushion spurge)
Geranium macrorrhizum 'Spessart' (bigroot
    geranium)
Geranium x oxonianum 'Claridge Druce'
    (cranesbill)
Geranium platypetalum (cranesbill)
Geranium sanguineum 'Album' (cranesbill)
Geranium sanguineum striatum (cranesbill)
Hosta 'Golden Tiara'
Hosta 'Shade Fanfare'
Iberis sempervirens (candytuft)

Lamium maculatum 'White Nancy'
(dead nettle)
Lamprocapnos spectabilis 'Alba' (white
bleeding-heart)
Ligularia stenocephala 'The Rocket' (ligularia)
Lunaria annua (honesty, money plant)
Macleaya cordata (coral plume poppy)
Meconopsis cambrica (welsh poppy)
Melissa officinalis (lemon balm)
Mertensia virginica (Virginia bluebells)
Monarda didyma, in variety (bee balm)
Nepeta 'Six Hills Giant' (catmint)
Origanum vulgare (marjoram)
Origanum vulgare 'Aureum' (golden-leaved
oregano)
Paeonia 'Early Windflower'
Paeonia 'Felix Crousse'
Paeonia 'Festiva Maxima'
Paeonia 'Roselette'
Paeonia 'Sarah Bernhardt'
Papaver orientale (Oriental poppy)
Pulmonaria 'Roy Davidson'
Pulmonaria angustifolia (lungwort)
Sagina subulata (pearlwort)
Sedum spurium 'Dr. John Creech'
(stonecrop)
Sempervivums, in variety (hens and chicks)
Tanacetum parthenium (feverfew)
Thalictrum rochebrunianum (meadow rue)
Thymus minus (thyme)
Tradescantia x andersoniana (spiderwort)
Valeriana officinalis (garden heliotrope)
Viola dissecta (violet)

■ BULBS

Allium christophii (star of Persia)
Asiatic lilies, in variety

Spring Garden

■ WOODY PLANTS

Buxus microphylla 'Green Mountain' (boxwood)
Cornus alternifolia (pagoda dogwood)
Cornus stolonifera (red-twigged dogwood)
Enkianthus campanulatus
Hydrangea paniculata 'Tardiva'
Kalmia latifolia (mountain laurel)
Leucothoe fontanesiana (drooping leucothoe)
Magnolia 'Miss Honey Bee'

Malus 'Donald Wyman' (crab apple)
Pieris japonica 'Mountain Fire' (lily-of-the-
valley shrub)
Rhododendron 'Molly Fordham'
Rhododendron mucronulatum 'Cornell Pink'
(Cornell Pink azalea)
Thuja occidentalis 'Smaragd' (emerald green
arborvitae)
Viburnum sargentii 'Onondaga' (Sargent
viburnum)
Vinca minor 'Bowles' (periwinkle)

■ HERBACEOUS PERENNIALS

Anemone tomentosa 'Robustissima' (grape-
leaved anemone)
Aquilegia alpina (alpine columbine)
Aquilegia alpina hybrids
Aruncus dioicus (goatsbeard)
Asarum canadensis (American ginger)
Asarum europaeum (European ginger)
Astilbe taquetti 'Superba'
Astilbes, in variety
Astrantia major (masterwort)
Athyrium nipponicum 'Pictum' (Japanese
painted fern)
Brunnera macrophylla
Campanula glomerata 'Joan Elliott'
Campanula glomerata 'Superba'
Chasmanthium latifolium (wild oats)
Convallaria majalis (lily-of-the-valley)
Digitalis ferruginea (foxglove)
Digitalis purpurea
Doronicum grandiflorum (leopard's bane)
Doronicum orientale 'Magnificum'
Epimedium grandiflorum 'White Queen'
Epimedium x rubrum
Epimedium x versicolor "Sulphureum"
Geranium x magnificum (cranesbill)
Geranium renardii 'Philippe Vapelle' (cranesbill)
Geranium sanguineum 'Album' (cranesbill)
Hosta 'Albomarginata'
Hosta 'Golden Tiara'
Hosta 'Krossa Regal'
Iris pseudacorus (yellow flag iris)
Iris sibirica, in variety (Siberian Iris)
Lamium galeobdolon 'Florentinum'
(yellow archangel)
Lamprocapnos spectabilis 'Alba'
(white bleeding-heart)
Ligularia dentata 'Desdemona'

*Acer pseudosieboldianum—**fall foliage.***

Lysimachia nummularia 'Aurea'
(yellow-leaved creeping Jenny)
Muscari armeniacum 'Cantab' (grape
hyacinth)
Myrrhis odorata (sweet cicely)
Osmunda regalis (royal fern)
Penstemon fruticosus 'Purple Haze'
(beard-tongue)
Persicaria polymorpha
Primula denticulata (drumstick primrose)
Primula japonica (candelabra primrose)
Pulmonaria angustifolia, in variety (lungwort)
Rodgersia pinnata
Salvia glutinosa (Jupiter's distaff)
Sanguinaria canadensis 'Flore Pleno'
(double bloodroot)
Sidalcea 'Elsie Heugh' (checker mallow)
Sidalcea 'Party Girl' (checker mallow)
Thalictrum rochebrunianum (meadow rue)
Thermopsis villosa (Carolina lupine)
Tiarella 'Slick Rock' (foamflower)
Tiarella cordifolia (foamflower)
Uvularia grandiflora (merrybells, bellwort)
Veronica nummularia (speedwell)

■ BULBS

Daffodils, in variety, including *Narcissus*
'King Alfred' and 'Louise de Coligny'

Pool Garden / Daylily Bank

■ TREES

Abies balsamea (balsam fir)

Abies koreana (korean fir)

Acer japonicum 'Aconitifolium' (Japanese maple)

Acer platanoides 'Crimson King' (crimson king Norway maple)

Acer saccharum (sugar maple)

Acer tataricum ginnala (amur maple)

Betula papyrifera (white birch)

Cladrastis kentuckea (yellowwood)

Fraxinus pennsylvanica (northern ash)

Nyssa sylvatica (tupelo)

Phellodendron amurense (cork tree)

Robinia pseudoacacia (black locust, indigenous to the area)

Salix alba (white willow)

Salix alba vitellina (yellow willow)

Syringa reticulata (Japanese tree lilac)

Thuja occidentalis 'Smaragd' (emerald green arborvitae)

Tsuga canadensis (eastern hemlock)

Ulmus 'Regal' (regal elm)

■ SHRUBS AND VINES

Abies balsamea 'Nana' (dwarf balsam fir)

Actinidia kolomikta 'Arctic Beauty' (kiwi vine)

Akebia quinata (five-leaved akebia)

Cornus stolonifera 'Cardinal'

Cornus stolonifera 'Flaviramea' (golden-twigged dogwood)

Cornus stolonifera 'Variegata' (variegated red osier)

Euonymus fortunei

Fothergilla gardenii (witch alder)

Hydrangea parniculata 'Unique'

Juniperus virginiana 'Grey Owl' (juniper)

Lonicera x brownii 'Dropmore Scarlet' (Dropmore Scarlet honeysuckle)

Lonicera x tellmaniana (Tellman's honeysuckle)

Pinus mugo (mugho pine)

Salix integra 'Hakuro-nishiki' (variegated willow), shrub form

Salix integra 'Hakuro-nishiki' (variegated willow), tree form

Syringa patula 'Miss Kim' (lilac)

Taxus canadensis (American yew)

Taxus x media 'Hicksii' (Hicks yew)

Thuja occidentalis (dark American arborvitae)

Thuja occidentalis 'Woodwardii' (globe arborvitae)

Viburnum x burkwoodii (burkwood viburnum)

Viburnum lantana 'Mohican' (wayfaring tree)

Viburnum plicatum 'Mariesii' (doublefile viburnum)

Viburnum sargentii 'Onondaga' (Sargent viburnum)

■ HERBACEOUS PERENNIALS

Ajuga reptans 'Gaiety' (bugleweed)

Alchemilla mollis (lady's mantle)

Amsonia tabernaemontana (bluestar)

Anemone tomentosa 'Robustissima' (grape-leaved anemone)

Angelica atropurpurea

Asarum europaeum (European ginger)

Brunnera macrophylla

Calamagrostis acutiflora 'Karl Foerster' (feather reed grass)

Campanula takesimana (bellflower)

Chasmanthium latifolium (wild oats)

Delosperma nubigenum

Eupatorium maculatum 'Gateway' (Joe Pye weed)

Euphorbia 'Firecracker'

Galium odoratum (sweet woodruff)

Hens and chicks, in variety

Hosta 'Ellerbroek'

Hosta 'Gold Drop'

Hosta 'Hadspen Blue'

Hosta 'Krossa Regal'

Hosta 'Mediovariegata'

Hosta 'Sum and Substance'

Hosta 'Sun Power'

Hosta 'Tokudama Flavocircinalis'

Hosta grandiflora

Hosta sieboldii 'Albomarginata'

Hylotelephium 'Autumn Joy'

Hylotelephium 'Vera Jameson'

Kirengeshoma palmata (yellow waxbells)

Lysimachia nummularia 'Aurea' (yellow-leaved creeping Jenny)

Oenothera fruticosa (evening primrose)

Phlox divaricata (woodland phlox)

Phlox divaricata 'Dirgo Ice'

Sasa veitchii (kuma bamboo grass)

Sedum pachyclados (stonecrop)

Sedum spurium 'Dr. John Creech'

Sempervivum tectorum (hens and chicks)

Stachys byzantina 'Primrose Heron' (lamb's ears)

Thymus x citriodorus (lemon thyme)

Thymus pseudolanuginosus 'Hall's Variety' (Hall's woolly thyme)

Fothergilla gardenii —*fall foliage.*

Thymus serpyllum

Tiarella cordifolia (Foamflower)

Tricyrtis latifolia (toad lily)

Fields

■ TREES

Cercidiphyllum japonicum (katsura)

Ginkgo biloba 'Saratoga' (Saratoga ginkgo)

Pinus aristata (bristlecone pine)

Quercus palustris (pin oak)

Quercus robur 'Fastigiata' (fastigiate English oak)

The Spring Garden is where it all began back in March 1984.

APPENDIX C:
Initial Bloom Dates for Some Flowering Plants in Vermont

THE FOLLOWING LIST is based on the initial bloom date for our flowering plants. Bloom time from year to year and even from one area of the garden to another is not always the same because of sun/shade conditions, or wind exposure, or any number of other variables. *Geranium phaeum* in the full-shade garden by the gazebo blooms five to seven days later than the *G. phaeum* in partial sun in the perennial borders. The fact that a certain type of plant blooms at different times under different conditions can work to your advantage. We planted snowdrops, for example, along a south-facing stone in full sun, where they bloom many days before those in the woodland where some shade passes over them throughout the day. In this way you can spread out the blooms of many plants that can tolerate both shade and some sun.

Another issue affecting the following list is that spring 2003, for example, started relatively late, in part because snow was on the ground from late October (a heavy snow fell before all the leaves were off the trees) and stayed on the ground until late March. We then had a cool, even cold, and rainy May, which set many plants back at least two weeks as compared to spring 2002. (The *Phlox divaricata* in the Woodland Garden that peaked on May 10, 2002, peaked on May 29, 2003.) The rain then let up in mid-June; it got extremely hot for three weeks and we had virtually no rain. This heat and drought after so much rain and cold caused a burst of bloom.

Having said all this, the following list remains valuable for designing a garden in Zone 4, irrespective of the vicissitudes of weather in 2003. If you make your own list by noting plants in bloom in your own garden and those of others in your area, you will create an invaluable record that will help you design your garden for simultaneous bloom. Such lists are important if you intend to design gardens keyed to certain bloom times: the Spring Garden, the June Garden, the High Summer Garden, the Fall Garden.

Avoid designing a garden by going to a nursery and choosing plants that are in bloom. Plants in pots in a display yard in full sun may well bloom a full two weeks or more before those in the ground. Several factors cause potted plants in nursery display areas to bloom earlier than they will in your garden. Black plastic pots absorb heat from sunlight and hasten growth, and nursery owners provide optimum watering and fertilizing conditions to bring on bloom. Design your color combinations based on the bloom time of plants in the ground, not in pots.

Finally, we have had few problems with deer, so some plants in the following list might not be feasible in a garden with heavy deer browsing.

APRIL 16

Daphne mezereum (February daphne)
Galanthus elwesii (snowdrops)
Galanthus nivalis, in variety (snowdrops)

APRIL 20

Crocus chrysanthus, in variety
Crocus tommasinianus, in variety
Iris reticulata (rock garden iris)

APRIL 22

Eranthis hyemalis (winter aconite)
Narcissus: 'Hawera', 'Ice Follies', 'Ice Wings', 'Jet Fire', 'King Alfred', 'Louise de Coligny', 'Mount Hood', 'Passionale', 'Peeping Tom', 'Pheasant's Eye', 'Salome', 'Tete-a-Tete', 'Thalia', 'White Lion', among many others

APRIL 25

Primula denticulata, in variety (drumstick primrose)
Sanguinaria canadensis 'Flore Pleno' (double bloodroot)

Virginia bluebells (Mertensia virginica) *and daffodils.*

APRIL 27

Erica carnea, in variety (spring or snow heather)
Forsythia 'Northern Sun' and 'Meadowlark'
Pulmonaria 'Majesty' and 'Roy Davidson', among others (lungwort)

APRIL 28

Buxus koreana (Korean boxwood)

APRIL 29

Magnolia x soulangiana (saucer magnolia)
Mertensia virginica (Virginia bluebells)
Muscari armeniacum 'Cantab' (grape hyacinth)
Muscari azureum (grape hyacinth)
Primula veris 'Lutea', among others (cowslip)

APRIL 30

Dicentra eximia 'Snowdrift' (everlasting bleeding-heart)
Dicentra formosa 'Aurora' (western bleeding-heart)
Dicentra formosa 'Zestful' (everlasting bleeding-heart)
Epimedium grandiflorum 'White Queen' (barrenwort)
Epimedium x rubrum (barrenwort)

Erythronium americanum (trout lily)
Pachysandra procumbens (Allegheny spurge)
Prunus americana (wild plum)
Scilla bifolia (squill)
Vinca minor 'Bowles' (periwinkle)
Viola labradorica (Labrador violet)

MAY 3

Fritillaria meleagris (snake's head fritillary)
Rhododendron mucronulatum 'Cornell Pink'
    (Cornell Pink azalea)
Trillium viride (wood trillium)
Uvularia grandiflora (wild oats)
Viola dissecta (violet)

MAY 5

Euphorbia dulcis 'Chameleon' (purple-
    leaved spurge)
Euphorbia polychroma (cushion spurge)
Prunus x domestica (plum tree)
MAY 9

Epimedium x versicolor 'Sulphureum'
    (barrenwort)
Fritillaria persica (Persian fritillary)
Magnolia stellata (star magnolia)

MAY 10

Amelanchier canadensis (shadblow)

*Woodland phlox (*Phlox divaricata*), the whiter*
P.d. *'Dirgio Ice', and* Euphorbia polychroma.

Amelanchier stolonifera (stoloniferous
    shadblow)
Anemone japonica, in variety (candelabra
    primrose)
Leucojum aestivum 'Gravetye' (snowflakes)
Leucojum vernum (spring snowflakes)

MAY 13

Tulips, in pots: 'Angelique', 'Apricot Beauty',
    'Elizabeth Arden', 'Estella Rijnveld',
    'Flaming Parrot', 'Mrs. John T. Scheepers',
    'Passionale', 'Peach Blossom', 'Queen of
    Night', 'Queen of Sheba', 'Red Emperor',
    'White Emperor', among many others

MAY 14

Rhododendron 'Molly Fordham' (little-leaved
    rhododendron)
Syringa vulgaris hybrids, in variety (lilacs)

MAY 15

Arabis sturii (rockcress)
Asarum canadense (American ginger)
Asarum europaeum (European ginger)
Phlox divaricata (blue woodland phlox)
Phlox divaricata 'Dirgo Ice' (white woodland
    phlox)

MAY 15

Ajuga reptans 'Atropurpurea', 'Burgundy
    Glow', 'Caitlin's Giant', 'Gaiety', among
    others (bugleweed)
Anemone nemorosa 'Dwarf Lavender'
    (European wood anemone)
Brunnera macrophylla 'Variegata'
    (Siberian bugloss)
Fothergilla gardenii 'Mt. Airy' (witch alder)
Lamium maculatum 'White Nancy'
    (dead nettle)
Lamprocapnos spectabilis 'Alba'
    (white bleeding-heart)
Myosotis sylvatica 'Victoria Blue'
    (forget-me-mot)
Polemonium caeruleum (Jacob's ladder)
Polemonium caeruleum 'Brise D'Anjou'
Primula juliae (primrose)
Tiarella 'Slick Rock' and species (foamflower)
Veronica americana (bird's eye, speedwell)
Viburnum x burkwoodii 'Chenaulti'
    (Burkwood viburnum)

Acer pseudosieboldianum, Ajuga reptans
'Caitlin's Giant', Pulmonaria officinalis,
Phlox stolonifera *'Sherwood Purple'*.

Vinca minor 'Purpurea' (periwinkle)
Waldsteinia ternata (Siberian barren
    strawberry)

MAY 17

Glaucidium palmatum

MAY 18

Acer pseudosieboldianum (false Siebold maple)
Aquilegia canadensis and hybrids
    (native columbine)
Malus baccata and *M. floribunda* hybrids:
    'Adams', 'Donald Wyman', 'Prairiefire',
    'Royalty', Sugar Tyme® (crab apples)
Rhododendron 'Aglo' (little-leaved
    rhododendron)

MAY 19

Malus pumila (standard apple tree)

MAY 21

Allium aflatunense (flowering onion)
Berberis thunbergii 'Kobold' (dwarf
    Japanese barberry)
Convallaria majalis (lily-of-the-valley)
Convallaria majalis 'Aureo-variegata'
    (variegated lily-of-the-valley)

Kerria japonica 'Variegata' (Japanese rose)
Rhododendron yedoense 'Poukhanense' (azalea)
Viburnum dentatum (arrowwood)
Viburnum lantana 'Mohican' (wayfaring tree)

MAY 22

Actaea rubra (red baneberry)
Berberis thunbergii 'Aurea' (yellow-leaved
   barberry)
Packera aurea (golden groundsel)
Phlox stolonifera 'Blue Ridge', 'Bruce's
   White', 'Home Fires', 'Sherwood Purple'
   (creeping phlox)
Prunus x cistena (purple-leaved sand cherry)
Sedum middendorffianum (stonecrop)
Sedum ternatum (stonecrop)

MAY 24

Arisaema triphyllum (jack-in-the-pulpit)
Fragaria X 'Lipstick' (barren strawberry)
Galium odoratum (sweet woodruff)
Spiraea x arguta 'Compacta' (garland spirea)
Ulmus 'Regal' (regal elm)

MAY 25

Caragana arborescens 'Pendula' (Siberian
   pea shrub)
Primula japonica, in variety (candelabra
   primrose)
Vaccinium corymbosum, in variety
   (highbush blueberry)
Viburnum x rhytidophyllum (leatherleaf
   viburnum)

*Feverfew (*Tanancitum parthenium*), Iris
'David' and the red field poppy (*Papaver
rhoeas*).

MAY 27

Doronicum orientale 'Magnificum'
   (leopard's bane)
Jeffersonia diphylla (twinleaf)
Lamium galeobdolon 'Florentinum'
   (yellow archangel)
Rhododendron indicum, in variety
Trollius chinensis 'Golden Queen'
   (globeflower)
Viburnum carlesii (mayflower)

*Mullein (*Verbascum chaixii*) and foxglove
(*Digitalis purpurea*).

MAY 30

Centaurea montana (mountain bluet)
Geranium phaeum 'Samobor' (mourning
   widow)
Meconopsis cambrica (Welsh poppy)
Paeonia 'Roselette' (herbaceous peony)
Penstemon fruticosus 'Purple Haze'
   (beard-tongue)
Syringa 'Tinkerbelle'™ (lilac)
Syringa x chinensis 'Lilac Sunday'
Viburnum prunifolium (black haw)

JUNE 3

Aquilegia caerulea (blue columbine)
Cerastium tomentosum (snow-in-summer)
Geranium 'Johnson's Blue' (cranesbill)
Geranium endressii 'Wargrave Pink'
   (cranesbill)

*Geranium 'Brookside' and sea holly (*Eryngium
planum *'Blaukappe')*

Geranium macrorrhizum 'Ingwersen's
   Variety' (bigroot geranium)
Hemerocallis lilioasphodelus (lemon lily)
Myrrhis odorata (sweet cicely)
Paeonia 'Windflower'
Podophyllum peltatum (mayapple)
Rheum palmatum 'Atrosanguineum'
   (puple-leaved rhubarb)
Symphytum officinale (comfrey)

JUNE 6

Magnolia 'Miss Honey Bee'

JUNE 7

Amsonia hubrechtii (bluestar)
Armoracia rusticana 'Variegata' (variegated
   horseradish)
Astrantia major 'Ruby Cloud' (masterwort)
Baptisia australis (false indigo)
Cornus alternifolia (pagoda dogwood)
Cornus sanguinea 'Winter Flame'
   (blood-twig dogwood)
Cornus stolonifera 'Baileyi' (Bailey's
   red-twigged dogwood)
Cornus stolonifera 'Flaviramea' (yellow-
   twigged dogwood)
Hesperis matronalis (sweet rocket)
Heuchera sanguinea, in variety (coralbells)

Artemisia *'Silver Queen' and foxglove*
(Digitalis ambigua*)*.

Hyacinthoides hispanica (Spanish bluebells)
Lamium galeobdolon 'Herman's Pride'
    (yellow archangel)
Nepeta 'Six Hills Giant' (catmint)
Papaver orientale, in variety, including
    'Elizabeth' (Oriental poppies)
Rhododendron catawbiense, in variety
Tradescantia virginiana 'Caerulea'
    (spiderwort)
Viburnum plicatum 'Mariesii' (doublefile
    viburnum)
Wisteria 'Aunt Dee'

JUNE 8

Acer tataricum ginnala 'Compacta'
    (amur maple)
Amsonia tabernaemontana (bluestar)
Campanula glomerata 'Joan Elliott'
    (bellflower)
Dictamnus albus (gas plant)
Dictamnus albus 'Purpureus'
Geranium x cantabrigiense 'Biokovo' (cranesbill)
Geranium sanguineum striatum
    (cranesbill)
Iberis sempervirens 'Purity' (candytuft)
Lamium maculatum 'White Nancy'
    (dead nettle)
Ornithogalum umbellatum (star of Bethlehem)

Persicaria polymorpha (fleece plant)

JUNE 9

Actinidia kolomikta 'Arctic Beauty'
    (kiwi vine)
Verbascum 'Jackie' (mullein)
Verbascum chaixii

JUNE 13

Cornus alba 'Elegantissima Variegata'
    (variegated red-twigged dogwood)
Eryngium planum 'Blaukappe' (sea holly)
Iris: 'Alizes', 'Babbling Brook', 'Black as
    Night', 'Champagne Elegance', 'David',
    'Emperor's Delight', 'Purgatory', 'Role
    Model', 'Unforgetable Fire', among many
    others (bearded iris)
Iris pseudacorus (yellow flag iris)
Iris sibirica, in variety (Siberian iris)
Nectaroscordum siculum bulgaricum
    (Bulgarian allium)
Nepeta sibirica (Siberian catmint)
Herbaceous peony hybrids: 'Claudia', 'Felix
    Crousse', 'Festiva Maxima', 'President
    Roosevelt', 'Sarah Bernhardt', among
    many others
Valeriana officinalis (garden heliotrope)

*Fairy Wing poppies from Thompson and
Morgan, and mullein (* Verbascum chaixii*).*

Salvia verticillata *'Purple Rain' and pinks*
(Dianthus gratianopolitanus *'Bath's Pink')*.

JUNE 15

Angelica atropurpurea (giant angelica)
Chionanthus virginicus (fringetree)
Cranesbills: Geranium cinereum 'Ballerina',
    Geranium maculatum, Geranium x
    oxonianum 'Claridge Druce', Geranium
    platypetalum, Geranium praetense
    'Brookside', Geranium renardii, G.
    renardii 'Philippe Vapelle', Geranium san-
    guineum 'Album'
Hydrangea petiolaris (climbing hydrangea)
Philadelphus coronarius (mockorange)
Rodgersia pinnata 'Superba' (Rodger's
    flower)
Stephenandra incisa 'Crispa' (lace shrub)
Syringa patula 'Miss Kim' (lilac)

JUNE 18

Allium christophii (star of Persia)
Aruncus dioicus (goatsbeard)
Briza media (quaking grass)
Coreopsis grandiflora 'Early Sunrise'
    (tickseed)
Crambe cordifolia
Digitalis ferruginea (foxglove)
Kalmia latifolia (mountain laurel)
Leucothoe fontanesiana (drooping
    leucothoe)

Penstemon 'Bashful' (beard-tongue)
Physocarpus opulifolius 'Dart's Gold' (gold-leaved ninebark)
Physocarpus opulifolius Diabolo™ (purple-leaved ninebark)
Rosa 'Mary Queen of Scots'
Rosa glauca (purple-leaved rose)
Syringa villosa (late lilac)
Veronica 'Crater Lake Blue' (speedwell)

JUNE 19

Alchemilla alpina (alpine lady's mantle)
Alchemilla mollis (lady's mantle)
Anchusa capensis 'Blue Bird' (alkanet, bugloss)

*The white blooms of giant kale (*Crambe cordifolia*) with red field poppies (*Papaver rhoeas*).*

Campanula glomerata 'Odessa'
Campanula latifolia 'Macrantha' (bellflower)
Cladrastis kentuckea (yellowwood tree)
Dianthus 'Bath's Pink' (pinks)
Dianthus 'Ian'
Digitalis x mertonensis (foxglove)
Heuchera 'Chocolate Ruffles', 'Petite Pearl Fairy', 'Silver Streak' (coralbells)
Lonicera x brownii 'Dropmore Scarlet' (Dropmore Scarlet honeysuckle)
Lonicera prolifera (moonvine honeysuckle)

Phellodendron amurense (cork tree)
Rhododendron 'Pink and Sweet' (azalea)

JUNE 21

Achillea millefolium 'Summerwine' (yarrow)
Allium moly (lily leek)
Astilbe japonica 'Deutschland' (perennial spirea)
Carex grayi (sedge)
Lonicera x heckrottii 'Gold Flame' (goldflame honeysuckle vine)
Papaver: Fairy Wings type
Thymus pseudolanuginosis 'Hall's Variety' (Hall's woolly thyme)
Thymus serpyllum (mother-of-thyme)

JUNE 23

Aruncus dioicus 'Kneiffii' (goatsbeard)
Heuchera 'Amethyst Myst' (coralbells)
Heuchera 'Pewter Veil'
Sedum kamtschaticum ellacombeanum (stonecrop)
Sedum spurium 'Dr. John Creech'

JUNE 25

Allium nigrum (flowering onion)
Campanula 'Elizabeth' (bellflower)
Campanula glomerata 'Superba' (clustered bellflower)
Digitalis grandiflora ambigua (foxglove)
Digitalis purpurea, in variety
Festuca glauca 'Elijah Blue' (blue fescue)
Filipendula vulgaris 'Grandiflora' (meadowsweet)
Hosta sieboldiana 'Elegans'
Lychnis chalcedonica (Maltese cross)
Matricaria recutita (sweet false chamomile)
Oenothera fruticosa (sundrops)
Penstemon digitalis 'Husker's Red' (beard-tongue)
Rosa 'William Baffin'
Salvia verticillata 'Purple Rain'
Sedum acre (stonecrop)
Sedum ramtschaticum 'Weihenstephaner Gold' (stonecrop)
Stachys macrantha 'Superba' (betony)
Syringa reticulata (Japanese tree lilac)

JUNE 28

Allium caeruleum (flowering onion)

Anthemis tinctoria 'Kelwayi' and A. t. 'E. C. Buxton' (golden marguerite)
Calamagrostis acutiflora 'Karl Foerster' (feather reed grass)
Campanula persicifolia 'Alba' and C. p. 'Blue' (peach-leaved bellflower)
Clematis 'Henryi'
Hosta 'Blue Shadows'
Hosta 'Sagae' (H. fluctuans 'Variegata')
Knautia macedonica
Lysimachia nummularia 'Aurea' (creeping Jenny, moneywort)
Stachys byzantina, 'Helene Von Stein', 'Primrose Heron', 'Silver Carpet' (lamb's ears)

JUNE 29

Echinops bannaticus 'Blue Glow' (globe thistle)
Geranium psilostemon (cranesbill)

JUNE 30

Cephalaria gigantea (giant cabious)
Coreopsis verticillata 'Zagreb' (tickseed)
Hemerocallis 'Happy Returns', and first of early midseason daylilies
Malva alcea fastigiata (rose mallow)

*Shasta daisy (*Leucanthemum x superbum *'Becky') and old-fashioned single hollyhocks (*Alcea rosea*).*

Ruta graveolens (common rue)
Thermopsis villosa (Carolina thermopsis)

JULY 1

Heliopsis helianthoides 'Summer Sun'
  (heliopsis)

JULY 3

Clematis recta grandiflora (erect clematis)
Papaver rhoeas (field poppy)
Papaver somniferum (poppy)

JULY 4

Hosta 'Aureomarginata'
Thalictrum kiusianum (dwarf meadow rue)

JULY 6

Alcea rosea 'Nigra' (black hollyhock)
Astilbe x arendsii 'Diamond'
Astilbe x arendsii 'Erika'
Astilbe x arendsii 'Fanal'
Astilbe japonica 'Deutschland'
Astilbe rosea 'Peach Blossom'
Coreopsis verticillata (tickseed)
Hosta 'Golden Tiara'
Inula helenium (elecampane)

Variegated Japanese silver grass
(Miscanthus sinensis *'Variegatus'*) *with*
*meadow rue (*Thalictrum rochebrunianum)
growing up through it.

Lavandula angustifolia 'Hidcote' (lavender)
Monarda 'Raspberry Wine' (bee balm)
Sambucus canadensis (American
  elderberry)
Sambucus racemosa 'Sutherland Gold'
  (yellow-leaved elderberry)
Sedum sexangulare (stonecrop)
Stewartia pseudocamellia (Japanese
  stewartia)
Teucrium chamaedrys (germander)

JULY 7

Alcea rosea, in variety (hollyhock)
Coreopsis verticillata 'Moonbeam' (tickseed)
Hosta 'Betcher's Blue'
Hosta 'Sum and Substance'
Leucanthemum x superbum 'Becky'
  (Shasta daisy)
Spiraea japonica 'Anthony Waterer' (Anthony
  Waterer spirea)

JULY 8

Macleaya cordata (coral plume poppy)
Rudbeckia fulgida speciosa (gloriosa daisy)

JULY 10

Thalictrum rochebrunianum (meadow rue)

JULY 13

Filipendula rubra (queen-of-the-prairie)
Ligularia stenocephala 'The Rocket'

JULY 18

Astrantia major 'Rosea' (masterwort)
Astrantia major 'Ruby Cloud'
Eryngium alpinium 'Donard Variety'
  (sea holly)
Eryngium planum 'Blaukappe' (blue cap
  sea holly)
Sidalcea 'Elsie Heugh' and 'Party Girl'
  (checker mallow)

JULY 19

Clematis paniculata (fall-blooming clematis)
Dipsacus fullonum (teasel)
Hypericum frondosum 'Sunburst'
  (St. Johnswort)

JULY 20

Campanula 'Elizabeth' (bellflower)

Miscanthus sinensis *'Variegatus' with the*
flower of Thalictrum rochebrunianum.

Daylilies, everywhere
Filipendula rubra 'Venusta' (queen-of-
  the-prairie)
Veronica 'Sunny Border Blue' (speedwell)

JULY 24

Achillea 'Coronation Gold' (yarrow)
Hosta 'Krossa Regal'
Stokesia laevis 'Blue Danube' (Stoke's aster)

JULY 25

Astilbe simplicifolia 'Ostrich Plume'
Campsis radicans (trumpet vine)
Echinacea paradoxa (yellow coneflower)
Echinacea purpurea 'Bravado' (purple
  coneflower)
Echinacea purpurea Kim's Knee High®
  (purple coneflower)
Echinacea purpurea 'Magnus' (purple
  coneflower)
Hosta 'Blue Cadet', and many other hostas
Sagina subulata (pearlwort)
Sedum spurium 'Fuldaglut' (stonecrop)

JULY 26

Gentiana septemfida (crested gentian)
Platycodon grandiflorus 'Fuji Blue', 'Fuji
  White', and 'Shell Pink' (balloon flower)

JULY 28

Catananche caerulea (cupid's dart)
Daylilies, throughout
Gypsophila paniculata (baby's breath)
Hosta 'Sun Power'
Hydrangea arborescens 'White Dome'
Hydrangea paniculata
Hydrangea paniculata 'Unique'

JULY 30

Artemisia lactiflora 'Guizho' (wormwood)
Daylilies, throughout
Ligularia dentata 'Othello'
Lilium lancifolium (tiger lily)
Lobelia cardinalis 'Alba' (white cardinal flower)
Lysimachia clethroides (gooseneck
   loosestrife)
Phlox maculata 'Miss Lingard' (garden
   phlox)
Phlox paniculata 'David' (garden phlox)
Solidago rugosa 'Fireworks' (goldenrod)
Veronicastrum virginicum (culver's root)

*Silver feather maiden grass (*Miscanthus
sinensis *'Silberfeder'), purple-leaved barberry
(*Berberis thunbergii *'Atropurpurea')—since
removed—and purple-leaved snakeroot
(*Cimicifuga ramosa *'Atropurpurea').*

*Joe Pye weed (*Eupatorium maculatum
'Gateway') with Phlox paniculata *'David'.*

AUGUST 3

Eupatorium maculatum 'Gateway'
   (Joe Pye weed)
Panicum virgatum 'Cloud Nine',
   'Heavy Metal', and 'Shenandoah'
   (switch grass)

AUGUST 5

Daylilies, throughout
Lobelia cardinalis (cardinal flower)
Lobelia siphilitica (blue cardinal flower)

AUGUST 10

Sanguisorba canadensis (burnet)

AUGUST 12

Anemone tomentosa 'Robustissima'
   (grape-leaved anemone)
Artemisia lactiflora (wormwood)
Clethra alnifolia (sweet pepperbush)

AUGUST 14

Aconitum carmichaelii 'Arendsii'
   (monkshood)
Helenium 'Riverton Beauty' (sneezeweed)
Hosta 'Royal Standard'

AUGUST 20

Chelone lyonii (turtlehead)
Helenium 'Moerheim Beauty' (sneezeweed)
Maackia amurensis

AUGUST 22

Deschampsia caespitosa (tussock grass)

AUGUST 29

Miscanthis oligostachys 'Purpurascens'
   (purple reed grass)

SEPTEMBER 5

Actaea simplex 'Atropurpurea' (purple-
   leaved snakeroot)
Hylotelephium 'Autumn Joy'
Hylotelephium spectabile 'Brilliant'

SEPTEMBER 9

Aster novae-angliae 'Andenken an Alma
   Potschke' (Michaelmas daisy)
Aster novae-angliae 'Woods Purple'
   (New England aster)
Aster novi-belgii 'Woods Pink' (New York
   aster)
Kirengeshoma palmata (yellow waxbells)

NOVEMBER 2

Hamamelis virginiana (witch hazel)

*Witch hazel (*Hamamelis virginiana*).*

We plant tulip bulbs in pots in October, store them over winter in the cold cellar, and bring the pots into the garden in late March.

APPENDIX D:
Planted Pots

EVERY LATE MAY we plant about fifty pots that go into our garden, some in full shade, some in dappled shade, some in blazing sun. Go into any good garden center yourself around Memorial Day and you will see a remarkable selection of annuals suitable for planting in containers. Even ten years ago the list of annuals you would find at a garden center was limited to petunias and marigolds, zinnias and fussy fuchsias. Now the whole world is your oyster: Egyptian starflowers and fragrant *Zaluzianskya*, *Gomphrena* from India and Mexican sunflower, *Salvia greggii* from Texas and African daisies.

Not only are there new tender annuals available, there are new ways of looking at hardy perennial and woody plants for containers. We planted the woody shrub Harry Lauder's walking stick (*Corylus avellana* 'Contorta') in a 24-inch-diameter pot.

An orange mum, a red-black coleus,
Artemisia *'Powis Castle', and Brazilian*
*button flower (*Centratherum intermedium*).*

In another, we set out a Japanese cutleaf maple far too tender to be planted in our Zone 4 garden here in southern Vermont. In a third pot of the same size, I planted two each of the hardy perennials *Hosta* 'Shade Fanfare' and *Kirengeshoma palmata*. (In winter, all of these go into our cold cellar where we water them once a month.)

Choosing the Pots

Virtually all the pots we have purchased over the years are terra-cotta. Though yours could be cast stone, fiberglass, or glazed ceramic, they must have a drainage hole in the bottom and should be from 16 to 24 inches in diameter across the top unless you are prepared to water smaller pots daily.

The Soil

We purchase 4-cubic-foot bags of Pro-Mix, a combination of peat moss, vermiculite, perlite, and fertilizers, from our local garden supply store. This same product is available across North America under different brand names. We use this product exclusively to fill all our pots. It's readily available, holds moisture well, and doesn't pack down the way topsoil does, so feeder rootlets can travel through it with ease, giving rise to healthy plants. Monthly fertilizing with a liquid fertilizer will see your plants flourishing throughout the growing season.

Choosing Plants: Upright, Mounding, Trailing

Now comes the fun part: choosing plants. If a specific plant you like is large and dramatic, you could fill an entire 18- to 24-inch pot with two or three specimens of the same variety. For example, I planted a 22-inch terra-cotta container with three 6-inch pots of the *coleus Solenostemon* 'Alabama Sunset'; by midsummer its orange-bronze-yellow foliage was 24 inches high and filled the pot. You could

Tulips galore.

also plant a large pot with two types of annuals. I've set three pink-flowering upright *Fuchsia* 'Billy Green' in the center of a pot, then surrounded them with five trailing blue Australian fan flower (*Scaevola aemula* 'New Wonder').

If you choose to combine three or more plants in a pot, a new principle emerges. Choose at least one trailing plant, to flow over the side of the pot, and at least one mounding plant, to fill in the space between the crown of the trailer up to about the middle of at least one upright plant growing among the mounding plants. When you go to a garden center, make lists of each type—trailing, mounding, upright—and choose plants whose flower and foliage colors complement one another. Then lay out possible combinations right on the ground at the nursery before deciding which plants to purchase.

Here's an example from our own garden. In late May, after all danger of frost had passed, I planted five 4-inch *Ageratum* 'Blue Horizon' (24 to 30 inches high by summer's end) in the center of a 24-inch-diameter terra-cotta pot. I then planted three different 6-inch, pink-flowering, scented-leaved geraniums around the ageratum. Around the perimeter of the pot I alternated three each of the trailing shocking pink Million Bells (*Calibracoa*) with the chartreuse-leaved licorice plant (*Helichrysum petiolare* 'Limelight'). The result was a striking blue-pink-chartreuse combination.

Maintenance of Pots

What we have not mentioned about all the plants above is that they are low or no maintenance and require infrequent or no deadheading. During the growing season (May to mid-September here) I deadhead the ageratum three or four times, pull off spent flower heads from the geraniums as I'm walking by, and cut back the *Scaevola* and *Petunia integrifolia* mercilessly to within 8 to 10 inches of the roots when they get too leggy. Other than that, I simply water and fertilize.

On the other hand, there are several

Starting from upper left: Coleus ***'Gold Bound',*** Coleus ***'Golden Bedder',*** Plectranthus fosteri ***'Green on Green',*** Argyranthemum ***'Chelsea Girl',*** Agastache ***'Firebird',*** Centranthemum intermedium, Fucshia ***'Billy Green'.***

annuals we wouldn't do without that require frequent deadheading, such as *Argyranthemum* and phlox of sheep.

Common names vary across North America; those I show below derive from *Hortus Third*, though common names in your area may vary. Given the ever-changing nature of taxonomy and nomenclature, I have done my best to record the most up-to-date binomials for the plants listed here.

Pots for Sun, Planted Memorial Day 2003

■ 9-INCH POT

1 *Pennisetum setaceum* 'Rubrum' (red-leaved fountain grass)

■ 12-INCH POT

1 *Cleome* 'Linde Armstrong'
1 *Ipomoea batatas* 'Blackie' (black-leaved sweet potato vine)
2 *Scaevola aemula* 'New Wonder'

2 *Arctotis x hybrida* 'Flame' (African daisy)
3 *Origanum* 'Kent Beauty'

1 *Artemisia* 'Powis Castle'
1 *Oxalis vulcanicola*
1 *Salvia coccinea* 'Cherry Blossom'

3 *Petunia* Surfina Hybrids® 'Sky Blue'
1 *Strobilanthes dyeranus* (Persian shield)

2 *Alternanthera dentata* 'Rubiginosa' (indoor clover)
3 *Pelargonium sidoides* (species geranium)

■ 14-INCH POT

3 *Streptocarpella* 'Concord Blue'
1 *Strobilanthes dyeranus* (Persian shield)

1 *Pennisetum setaceum* 'Rubrum' (red-leaved fountain grass)
1 *Solenostemon* 'Dark Heart' (coleus)
1 *Solenostemon* 'Kiwi Fern' (coleus)

2 *Cleome* 'Linde Armstrong'
2 *Helichrysum petiolatum* 'Variegata'

Starting from lower left: Helichrysum petiolare ***'Limelight',*** Salvia farinacea ***'Victoria Blue',*** Phormium ***'Bronze Baby',*** Anisodontea scabra ***(in the background),*** and a red-black coleus.

(licorice plant)
1 *Salvia discolor*

1 *Artemisia* 'Powis Castle'
1 *Centrantherum punctatum* (Brazilian button flower)
1 *Pelargonium* 'Royale' (Balcon Series) (geranium)
1 *Solenostemon* 'Midnight Red' (coleus)

1 *Agastache* 'Peach'
2 *Agastache barberi* 'Firebird'
1 *Argyranthemum* 'Chelsea Girl'
1 *Helichrysum petiolatum* 'Variegata' (licorice plant)
2 *Petunia* 'Supertunia Red'

■ 16-INCH POT

1 *Ipomoea batatas* 'Marguarite' (chartreuse-leaved sweet potato vine)
1 *Salvia gauranitica* (salvia) (replaced with *Chrysanthemum* 'Helen' on Labor Day)

Hens and chicks, in variety

1 *Argyranthemum* 'Chelsea Girl'
2 *Helichrysum petiolatum* 'Variegata'
 (licorice plant)
3 *Scaevola aemula* 'New Wonder'

2 *Argyranthemum* 'Butterfly' (replaced with
 Chrysanthemum 'Helen' on Labor Day)
3 *Helichrysum petiolare* 'Limelight' (licorice
 plant)
2 *Heliotropium* 'Fragrant Delight' (heliotrope)

■ **18-INCH POT**

3 *Origanum dictamnus* (dittany of Crete)
2 *Salvia discolor*

1 *Anisodontea capensis*
1 *Cordyline australis* 'Red Sensation'
2 *Helichrysum petiolare* 'Limelight' (licorice
 plant)
3 *Salvia farinacea*
1 *Solenostemon* 'Inky Pink' (coleus)

1 *Anisodontea capensis*
1 *Phormium* 'Lancer'
5 *Salvia farinacea*
1 *Solenostemon* 'Inky Pink' (coleus)

1 *Pennisetum setaceum* 'Rubrum'

*Angel's trumpet (*Brugmansia arborea*).*

(red-leaved fountain grass)
2 *Petunia* Surfina Hybrids® 'Lime'
1 *Solenostemon* 'Merlot' (coleus)

■ **22-INCH POT**

1 *Artemisia* 'Powis Castle'
1 *Fuchsia* 'Billy Green'
2 *Heliotropium* 'Fragrant Delight'
5 *Nasturtium* 'Empress of India'
1 *Salvia discolor*

■ **24-INCH POT**

3 *Agastache barberi* 'Firebird'
3 *Calibrachoa* 'Terra-Cotta' (Million
 Bells Hybrids®)

2 *Fuchsia* 'Gartenmeister Bonstedt'
5 *Phacelia campanularia* (California bluebell)
2 *Sanvitalia* 'Sunbini'
1 *Solenostemon* 'Kingswood Torch' (coleus)
2 *Torenia* 'Summer Wave Blue'

3 *Agastache barberi* 'Firebird'
3 *Angelonia* 'Carita Purple'
1 *Helichrysum petiolare* 'Limelight'
 (licorice plant)
2 *Helichrysum petiolare* 'Variegata'
 (licorice plant)

Other Pots for Full Sun Planted Over the Years

■ **20-INCH POT**

2 *Felicia amelloides* 'Variegata'
2 *Fuchsia* 'Gartenmeister Bonstedt'
3 *Helichrysum petiolatum* 'Variegata'
 (licorice plant)

1 *Anisodontea scabrosa* (African mallow)
3 *Heliotropium* 'Fragrant Delight'
2 *Petunia* 'Supertunia Sun Stryker'
1 *Sutera* 'Snowstorm' (bacopa)

1 *Artemisia* 'Powis Castle'
4 *Calibrachoa* 'Trailing Pink'
4 *Streptocarpella* 'Good Hope'

The perennial Geranium platypetalum *with the annual* Argyranthemum *'Butterfly'.*

■ **22-INCH POT**

3 *Nepeta x faassenii* 'Walker's Low' (catmint)
3 *Petunia integrifolia*
1 *Tibouchina urvilleana* 'Edwardsii'

2 *Argyranthemum* 'Butterfly'
2 *Browallia americana* (amethyst flower,
 bush violet)
2 *Ipomoea batatas* 'Marguarite' (chartreuse-
 leaved sweet potato vine)
3 *Pentas lanceolata* 'Nova'

■ **24-INCH POT**

1 *Brugmansia* 'Sunray' (angel's trumpets)
6 *Heuchera* 'Stormy Seas'

Pots for Shade, Planted Memorial Day 2003

■ **10-INCH POT**

1 *Begonia x* tuberosa *hybrida* 'Illumination
 Hybrids' 'Apricot'
2 *Torenia* 'Summer Wave Blue'

Fuchsia *'Gartenmeister Bonstedt'* with a
red-leaved coleus.

■ 16-INCH POT

3 *Impatiens* 'Seashells Hybrids'
3 *X Streptocarpella*

■ 18-INCH POT

2 *Fuchsia* 'Amy Lye'
3 *Impatiens* 'Seashells Hybrids'

1 *Alocasia micholitziana* 'Frydek'
1 *Calocasia* 'Black Magic'

■ 22-INCH POT

1 *Ipomoea batatas* 'Marguarite'
   (chartreuse-leaved sweet potato vine)
2 *Solenostemon* 'CJ' (coleus)
2 *Torenia* 'Summer Wave Blue'

3 *Solenostemon* 'Alabama Sunset' (coleus)

1 *Begonia x hybrida* 'Illumination Hybrids'
   'Salmon Pink'
2 *Millium effusum* 'Aureum' (Bowles'
   golden grass)
5 *Torenia* 'Summer Wave Blue'

■ 24-INCH POT

6 *Impatiens* 'Seashells Hybrids'
2 *Millium effusum* 'Aureum' (Bowles'
   golden grass)

Annuals Planted in Flower Beds

Nicotiana 'White Perfume' (flowering tobacco)
Nicotiana knightiana
Nicotiana langsdorffii
Nicotiana sylvestris
Pentas 'Mars' (Egyptian starflower)
Salvia 'Indigo Spires'
Verbena bonariensis

Sources

■ CUSTOM-MADE POTS

Jeff Pentland Pottery
14 Ocean View Drive
Hartland, VT 05048
802 436-9122
pentlandpottery@aol.com

Jeff is English and highly trained. His beautiful hand-made terra-cotta pots are reasonably priced. Shipping is by arrangement, though he would love to see you at his old-fashioned wood-fired kiln in Vermont, nowhere near the ocean.

■ ANNUAL PLANTS

Avant Gardens
710 High Hill Road
Dartmouth, MA 02747
508 998-8819
avantgardensne.com

The Great Plant Company
PO Box 1041
New Hartford, CT 06057
800 441-9788
Fax: 860 379-8488
greatplants.com

Logee's Nursery
141 North Street
Danielson, CT 06790
888 330-8038
logees.com

APPENDIX E:
Herbs

THESE HERBS WERE PLANTED in the 8-inch-diameter Long Tom pots set into the Vermont Herb Garden. Common names vary across North America; those I show below derive from *Hortus Third*, though common names in your area may vary. Given the ever-changing nature of taxonomy and nomenclature, I have done my best to record the most up-to-date binomials for the plants listed here.

Anethum graveolens 'Bouquet' (dill)
Carum carvi (caraway)
Coriandrum sativum (Chinese parsley)
Foeniculum vulgare 'Bronze' (bronze fennel)
Laurus nobilis (sweet bay)
Lavandula dentata 'Lambikins' (lavender)
Lavandula multifida (fernleaf lavender)
Marrubium vulgare (horehound)
Melissa officinalis (lemon balm)
Mentha suaveolens 'Variegata' (pineapple mint)
Ocimum basilicum (sweet basil)
Origanum dictamnus (dittany of Crete)
Origanum majorana (sweet marjoram)
Origanum vulgare (Italian oregano)

Origanum vulgare 'Aureum' (golden marjoram)
Petroselinum crispum 'Banquet' (parsley)
Rosmarinus officinalis (rosemary)
Rosmarinus officinalis 'Prostratus' (trailing rosemary)
Salvia officinalis 'Aurea' (yellow-leaved sage)
Salvia officinalis 'Tricolor' (three-colored sage)
Stevia rebaudiana (stevia)
Tanacetum vulgare (tansy)
Tulbaghia violacea (society garlic)
Yucca filifera 'Golden Sword'

APPENDIX F:
Plants at Courtyard House

COMMON NAMES VARY across North America; those I show below derive from *Hortus Third*, though common names in your area may vary. Given the ever-changing nature of taxonomy and nomenclature, I have done my best to record the most up-to-date binomials for plants listed here.

■ TREES

Acer palmatum 'Issai-nishiki-momiji' (*Issai* means "feature develops in one year"; *nishiki* means "rough"; *momiji* means "maple")

Acer palmatum dissectum 'Garnet' (Japanese red-leaved maple)

Catalpa bignonioides 'Aurea' (yellow-leaved catalpa), coppiced

Robinia pseudoacacia 'Frisia' (yellow-leaved black locust)

■ SHRUBS

Aucuba japonica 'Variegata' (gold dust plant), in a pot

Buddleia davidii 'Black Knight' (butterfly bush)

Buxus sempervirens (boxwood)

Ceratostigma willmottianum (Chinese plumbago)

Choisya ternata (Mexican orange)

Cornus 'Norman Hadden'

Cotoneaster horizontalis, trained on a wall

Escallonia 'Gold Brian'

Euonymus japonicus 'Bravo', on a standard

Fuchsia magellanica 'Riccartonii'

Fuchsia magellanica 'Versicolor'

Ilex x altaclarensis 'Gold King' (yellow-leaved holly)

Ilex x altaclarensis 'Gold Queen' (yellow-leaved holly)

Lonicera nitida 'Baggesen's Gold' (yellow-leaved honeysuckle)

Photinia x fraseri 'Red Robin', in a pot

Phygelius 'Trewidden Pink'

Phygelius x rectus 'African Queen'

Pittosporum tenuifolium 'Gold Star', in a pot

Sarcococca hookeriana

Viburnum tinus

Weigela middendorffiana

Catalpa bignonioides *'Aurea' and* Acer palmatum *'Issai-nishiki-momiji'*.

■ VINES

Hedera helix (ivy)
Parthenocissus henryana (Virginia creeper)
Schizophragma hydrangeoides 'Roseum' (Japanese hydrangea vine)
Tropaeolum speciosum (Scottish flame vine)
Tropaeolum tuberosum 'Ken Aslet'
Wisteria sinensis

■ HERBACEOUS PERENNIALS

Aconitum napellus (monkshood)
Agastache barberi 'Firebird'
Alchemilla mollis (lady's mantle)
Arabis androsacea (rock cress)
Artemisia lactiflora 'Guizho' (wormwood)
Astilbe x Arendsii hybrids
Astrantia major 'Ghost'
Bergenia 'Bressingham'
Bergenia 'Wintermarchen'
Brunnera macrophylla 'Dawson's White'
Campanula persicifolia 'Blue' (bellflower)
Campanula poscharskyana
Centranthus ruber (lady's pin cushion)
Crocosmia citronella (montbretia)
Crocosmia solfaterre (montbretia)
Digitalis ferruginea (foxglove)
Digitalis lutea
Digitalis parviflora

Euonymous fortunei 'Argenteo-marginatus'
Euphorbia x martinii
Fragaria vesca 'Perpetual' (woodland strawberry), in pots
Gentiana septemfida
Geum 'Lady Stratheden'
Helleborus orientalis 'Hillier Hybrid' (hellebore)
Heuchera 'Plum Pudding' (coralbells)
Heuchera micrantha 'Persian Carpet'
Heucherella 'Kimono', in a pot
Hosta sieboldiana 'Elegans'
Kniphofia 'Torch Lily' (red hot poker)
Lamium maculatum 'White Nancy' (dead nettle)
Paeonia 'Sarah Bernhardt'
Papaver cambriensis (Welsh poppy)
Patrina gibbosa (gold valerian)
Pulmonaria 'Roy Davidson' (lungwort)
Sagina subulata 'Aurea'
Saxifraga cuscutiformis
Saxifraga rubrifolia
Saxifraga umbrosa 'Variegata' (variegated London Pride)
Sedum 'Gold Mound' (stonecrop)
Sedum spurium
Thymus 'Doone Valley' (thyme)
Tiarella 'Tigerstripe' (yellow-leaved foamflower)

Hakonechloa macra *'Aureola',* Carex petriei, *and* Carex buchananii.

Tiarella cordifolia *'Tigerstripe' and* Hakonechloa macra *'Aurea' bring the chartreuse color of* Robinia pseudoacacia *'Frisia' to ground level.*

Waldstenia ternata

■ ALPINES ALONG EDGE OF PATH

Acaena microphylla (New Zealand burr)
Erodium reichardii
Erodium x variabile 'Purple Haze'
Helianthemum 'Wisley Primrose' (rock rose)
Pratia pedunculata 'County Park'
Silene uniflora 'Druett's Variegated' (campion)

■ GRASSES

Carex buchananii (sedge)
Carex petriei
Hakonechloa macra 'Aureola' (Hakon grass)
Miscanthus sinensis 'Zebrinus' (zebra grass)
Molinia caerulea 'Variegata' (variegated moor grass)
Stipa gigantea, in a pot

■ FERNS

Asplenium scolopendrium (hart's tongue fern)
Asplenium trichomanes (maidenhair spleenwort)
Dryopteris affinis 'Crispa Gracilis'
Dryopteris erythrosora (Japanese rosy buckler fern)
Dryopteris filix-mas 'Crispa Cristata' (cristate male fern)
Polystichum setiferum 'Plumoso-multichum'

APPENDIX G:
Research and Garden Design

WHEN A CLIENT ASKS me to design a garden, I begin a process, the stages of which rarely change. The process I follow might well be the sequence you could follow as you design your own garden. First, I visit the site to meet the people, see the architecture, and walk the land. Once I have a good understanding of all three, a design sequence begins that involves distinct kinds of research: background research into the clients, their home, and its surrounding landscape; soft research to inspire overall design ideas; and technical research into appropriate plants and materials. Each of these stages helps me and the client focus on an increasingly clear image of what the overall garden will look like and how its parts will relate to the whole. Throughout, my role is to draw clients, architecture, and landscape together into one harmonious whole.

Background Research

The initial research for a landscape or garden design revolves around getting to know the clients. Do children or parents live with them? How is their home furnished? Is it formal or informal? What colors predominate? What kind of art, if any, do they appreciate? How will they use the garden? Are they sun or shade lovers? Will they maintain the garden themselves or hire help? Do they want to raise vegetables? Cut flowers? Do they want a swimming pool or tennis court? The list goes on, but the point is that a garden designer needs to know clients well and how they will live in and use their garden and its outdoor living spaces. Based on that research, I design a garden for them, not for myself.

I also look at the clients' house, because it is usually the center of the garden. Its age, style, materials, and lines are key sources of initial inspiration. Doors suggest the beginning of paths into the garden. Windows help the garden designer see views that call for framing or screening. The proportions and dimensions of exterior walls provide clues to the shape and size of an adjacent terrace, patio, or garden. The color of those walls might suggest a color for outdoor furniture, ornamentation, and garden structures as well as flower and foliage in the outdoor living spaces. The nature and volume of space between the house and garage or another outbuilding can provide clues to developing the space in light of how it will be used.

I walk the land to all boundary lines, with my clients and later without them, to fully understand the whole property: its dimensions and proportions relative to the house and its windows and doors and outdoor living spaces. I also want to understand the property's relationship to the neighbors and the nearby and distant natural world. What native plants abound, and what do they reveal about the soil and climate? Are there bedrock outcroppings? Boulders, sand, gravel? Water? Where are potential or existing view lines? Which areas are shaded? Sunny? Dry? Moist? What is ugly and what is beautiful? Which areas have spirit and which feel bland? What are the inherent qualities of each part of the property, and where are the rough boundary lines between each of them? I constantly ask myself two questions: What can I do in this area that I can't do anywhere else? And where will paths go that will help me link all of these disparate parts into one coherent whole along one easily understood itinerary?

Soft Research

With this background research in mind, I turn to sources to help me develop the overarching design ideas for the property. If I found boulders and bedrock, I think back to gardens I've visited that also had massive stones incorporated into the garden. If the property has striking views, I think of attractive treatments I've seen, both designed and naturally occurring.

Also useful here are books with design ideas that are timeless and universal, as well as more timely articles and images in recently published books and magazines, and my own collection of slides and photographs of nature and designed gardens. I look to photos of natural streams to see how to mimic nature when designing a garden stream. When considering how to site a garden sculpture, I go to photographs of gardens where the designer used sculpture to draw people along a series of connected paths. For ideas about how to create an appropriate outdoor sitting area near an eighteenth-century Vermont farmhouse, I may use images of historical gardens in New England, the Pacific Northwest, or Britain.

It is particularly important to visit gardens locally and around the world. Garden designers need to see firsthand the gardens of many traditions in a wide range of styles in a wide range of climates, cultures, and countries. Visiting historical and contemporary gardens and researching the designers who made them within specific cultural or historical traditions also helps inform the design process.

When visiting gardens, I always take my camera. Photographs are important sources of inspiration, valuable not only for design ideas but as records of plant combinations, juxtaposition of materials, garden designs around buildings, the location of terraces and patios, the use of furniture or painted surfaces, the uses to which boulders and bedrock can be put, and so on. These photographs must be cataloged to be useful, so I organize my slides in specific drawers for specific countries, each subdivided into regions of the country (for example, United States: Pacific Northwest, Southwest, Southeast, Midwest, Northeast). Then I file twenty-slide sheets alphabetically by garden name.

An up-to-date library is essential. Mine

includes books and magazines that keep me abreast of changes going on in England, Europe, and across America. Highly focused articles help me develop specific techniques or plant combinations. Books on cutting-edge design might challenge ideas I'd previously thought sacrosanct. Going to online booksellers is an easy way to research new titles. Images from my library also help clarify concepts that might be hard for clients to visualize as we develop ideas for their garden.

Indirect sources also inspire the designer. Classical music, fine painting, architecture, photography, and sculpture all have the power to excite my design sensibilities. Talking with other designers or attending design symposia are equally powerful but in different ways.

A deeper source of inspiration—childhood memories—surfaces at the most surprising times. The mossy boulders and bedrock outcroppings that punctuate the Connecticut woods, or the stone walls that bordered the orchards where I grew up certainly influence me. Part of my inspiration as a designer comes from paying attention to those deep memories.

Technical Research

Having developed the framework for a design, I turn to technical research to help me make good decisions regarding plants and materials, pots and furniture, ornaments and artifacts. Books and magazines, of course, are crucial, as are nursery catalogs. CD-ROMS are especially useful when making plant choices. They are infinitely more flexible and immediate than books for getting specific information regarding plant choice and combinations for specific hardiness zones, and it is handy to print out photographs for clients, or provide them with slide shows of selected plants right on a computer screen. For example, if I want to develop a list of Zone 4 pink-flowering shrubs that are 4 to 6 feet high for moist, shaded soil, I highlight the appropriate icons for each of those variables on the main page and up comes a list cross-referenced to background material and a photograph of each plant. These horticultural CD-ROMS are complemented by those in the landscape architecture field that provide instant digital access to construction details for hardscaping and planting techniques as well as estimating and costing information.

The Internet is a vast and instantaneous source of technical information. Select key words such as garden mulches, stone garden paving, garden furniture, landscape design, or stonemasons, and hundreds of entries appear on your screen, often including related organizations. Nurseries often have Web sites that contain important plant information.

Through the Internet, professional groups such as the Association of Professional Landscape Designers (APLD) have initiated sites where members can share design information and make suggestions regarding plant combinations and design alternatives to gardens pictured on their Web site. Chat rooms and similar Web sites that individual designers could develop among themselves provide a wide range of possibilities for shared research.

Cable and satellite television have also opened up a broad range of stations that carry valuable, timely gardening information.

Perhaps the most important research that any garden designer can do is in his or her own garden. It is in your own garden that you experiment at ground level. It provides you with knowledge that eventually informs and solidifies all other sources of inspiration and research.

This article first appeared in Natural Surfaces: Visual Research for Artists, Architects and Designers *by Judy Juracek (W. W. Norton, 2002).*

INDEX